Beating the Odds

Beating the Odds

Beating the Odds
Overcoming Life's Trials

**Frank Minirth, Ike Minirth,
with Georgia Minirth Beach
and Mary Alice Minirth**

BAKER BOOK HOUSE

Grand Rapids, Michigan 49516

Copyright 1987 by
Baker Book House

ISBN: 0-8010-6217-9

Second printing, June 1989

Printed in the United States of America

Scripture references not otherwise marked are from the *New American Standard Bible*, © 1960, 1962, 1963, 1971, 1972, 1973, 1975, 1977 by the Lockman Foundation. Those marked NIV are from the New International Version, © 1973, 1978, 1984 by International Bible Society. Used by permission of Zondervan Bible Publishers. References marked KJV are from the King James Version.

To
Olive ("Dollie") Minirth

Her children arise up,
and call her blessed;
her husband also,
and he praiseth her.

Proverbs 31:28

Contents

Acknowledgments

First, I would like to thank my sister, Georgia Minirth Beach, for recording Dad's story and helping him to write it. While I have been the one in the family to write several books, I truly believe that my sister is the one with the talent. Also, she has apparently inherited my father's gift of storytelling which, it seems, is almost a lost art today.

Second, I would like to thank my godly wife, Mary Alice Minirth, for directing me to this Bible passage which is the motivation behind *Beating the Odds*.

Listen, O my people, to my instruction;
Incline your ears to the words of my mouth.
I will open my mouth in a parable;
I will utter dark sayings of old,
Which we have heard and known,
And our fathers have told us.
We will not conceal them from their children,
But tell to the generation to come the praises of the
  LORD,

9

And His strength and His wondrous works that He
   has done.
For He established a testimony in Jacob,
And appointed a law in Israel,
Which He commanded our fathers,
That they should teach them to their children,
That the generation to come might know, *even* the
   children *yet* to be born,
That they may arise and tell *them* to their children,
That they should put their confidence in God,
And not forget the works of God,
But keep His commandments, . . .

Psalm 78:1–7

Our hearts' desire also is that our children (the
third generation) "should put their confidence in God,
and not forget the works of God."

Frank Minirth, M.D.

Introduction:
Why Do Trials Come?

Why do Christians have trials?
Why do I have trials?
These questions are ones familiar to many of us. Further questions arise, too.

Am I suffering because of God's discipline (Heb. 12:9, 10)?

Am I suffering because someone else has sinned (Hosea)?

Am I suffering so that God can be glorified (John 9:3)?

Am I suffering to keep down pride (2 Cor. 12:7)?

Am I suffering to later show what faith in God can do (Mark 5:34)?

Am I suffering to produce character and hope (Rom. 5:3–5)?

Am I suffering because of my ministry for Christ (2 Cor. 11:24–28)?

Am I suffering to produce endurance and completeness in the Christian life (James 1:2–4)?

The apostle Paul recorded these words which have brought comfort to many sufferers through the years:

And he said unto me, My grace is sufficient for thee: for my strength is made perfect in weakness. Most gladly therefore will I rather glory in my infirmities, that the power of Christ may rest upon me.

2 Cor. 12:9–10

We may be like Job and never know exactly why we suffer through trials. Yet it is sufficient to know that God is there; He is in control, and He does care.

Looking at my trials in retrospect, I do understand some of them now, at least to a degree. But I don't fully understand some of the trials that my father went through. About them I say with the apostle Paul, that I "see through a glass, darkly." With appreciation of the insights that God has given us and with a bit of humor, Dad, my wife, and I here reflect on some of our trials.

Part One is Dad's story, as recorded by my sister. It is a heart-tugging and romantic narrative. Like the story of Esther in the Bible, God is ever present behind the scenes. Dad's story begins in a bygone age when time was not so rushed, when one could relax in front of a crackling fire as the family gathered around. Those were gentler days when old-fashioned values and a God who was there in trials were an expected part of life.

Trials often continue from generation to generation. *Part Two* is my story of my trials. It's a bit more on the serious side, and, try as I might, it lacks some of the down-home flavor of Dad's story. However, I trust that by telling about my personal struggles I will be helping others.

Part Three is my wife's account of her struggles and trials as a daughter, wife, and mother. I sincerely appreciate her willingness to show such vulnerability.

Part Four contains several ideas for overcoming trials, indeed for beating the odds, which God has taught us through the years. Some in-depth studies on trials conclude the book.

I'm sure you too, from your experiences, could probably teach many people about suffering. You may have been through more than we have. Yet I trust that God will use what we have learned from our trials to His glory.

PART ONE

Trials of a Former Age

Ike Minirth with Georgia Minirth Beach

1

Boy Dog, the Fighter

When I got married and acquired me a wife, I also gained the possession of a dog. Having found just the "right" girl, I was doubtful I had found just the "right" dog! However, he was my wife's dog and, having been given to us with the blessings of my mother-in-law, how could I refuse?

They called him Boy Dog. He was a mongrel of sorts and his most distinguishing feature was a dark red, shaggy coat. A dog of great size, he weighed sixty to seventy pounds, and resembled an Irish Setter more than any other blood line. However, his head was much broader. His mighty chest, strong shoulders, and sturdy legs showed he must have had some German Shepherd ancestors.

This dog had not come without recommendations (and good ones they were, indeed). According to the family, this dog could do just about anything.

"He's a good stock dog, Ike," my brother-in-law, Charlie, boasted. "He knows just when to heel a horse or cow and will head 'em in just the right direction to bring 'em in."

"And he's sure not a goose or a chicken killer," my wife, Dollie, added. "I've never caught him sucking on an egg in his entire life."

The one thing they did warn me about was his temper. More often than not, he was known to be the instigator of a fight with other dogs; and likewise, he didn't take to strangers invading the premises.

"Once when this Fuller Brush salesman came to our house, Boy Dog almost took a leg off before I could get him calmed down," Charlie warned. "If he knows a body, though, he won't bother him."

It didn't take me long to find out that Boy Dog was a competitor. I owned a horse named Pearl. Whenever I'd get the chance and wasn't out working in the field, I'd ride her. Boy Dog liked to run along beside us, keeping an even pace with Pearl and carefully observing her every move. One day, as I mounted the saddle, I looked down at the dog; and he looked back up at me. He had his head cocked sideways, his ears twitching. His excited manner said, "Let's go."

"How about a race, Boy Dog," I said. The twinkle in his eyes told me that he understood my words.

"Giddyup, Pearl." The heel of my boot dug into the horse's side. Without a moment's hesitation, the dog took a mighty leap forward and we were on our way. As we raced along, I'd glance downward encouraging him along.

"That-a-boy, come on here, Boy Dog, give it all ya got," I yelled. That time I won the race, but that was only the first one. After he found out exactly what was expected of him, he always kept up with me. We would usually run the quarter-of-a-mile strip that lay from our house to the highway; and more often than not, he would be sitting there panting heavily when Pearl and I would reach the destination. He would look at me in a very satisfied manner again, cocking his right eye up toward me as if to say, "I beat you that time!" From that day on all I would have to say to him is, "Let's race, Boy Dog!"

Not long after Boy Dog became a part of our family, my wife and I purchased our first automobile. We got it at a real bargain, which perhaps explained its looks. It was a faded-out, black, stripped-down Chevy with a front windshield being the only glass part in it. Amusing as it was, the Chevy was our only way of going places. We would not be any prouder today of a Cadillac than we were then of that old stripped-down car.

My wife and I would ride in the front seat, and Boy Dog would occupy the back seat all by himself. When Dollie didn't go along, the dog would sit in the front seat with me.

Invitation to Fight

One day I needed to make a trip into town, and I knew that Boy Dog would enjoy the ride, because he was always eager to keep me company. I whistled for him, and he came running from around front of the house. He liked to sleep on an old meat block there that Mr. Taylor had given me when his grocery store had gone out of business.

"You keep an eye out for him, and don't let him get into any fights, you hear!" my wife warned.

"Don't you worry now. I'll watch out for him," I said (recalling very well that I'd been told once before that Boy Dog could take care of himself in a scrap).

When I stopped at the International Harvester place at the edge of town to purchase some new plow points, I commanded Boy Dog to "stay." When a huge, white bulldog appeared and walked over to the strip-down, sniffing the tires and growling, with his teeth bared and his fur bristling, little did I know how great a temptation this would be for Boy Dog. It was plain to see that the bulldog was inviting a fight, and it didn't take long for Boy Dog to accept the invitation.

Boy Dog took a single leap from the front seat, meeting his aggressor head-on. A continuous roar arose as the two angry dogs tumbled back and forth with a gnashing and snarling of teeth, each dog waiting for the right moment to grasp a deadly hold.

As I ran from the building to get a better look, the thought raced through my mind of how many times in such fights a bulldog is known to go for the throat, holding on without letting go until its victim lies motionless and dead. I reached down and picked up a nearby stick, ready to step in if need be; for this dog was heavier in weight than my dog, and I had heard of his reputation.

Going for the Paw

Never having seen Boy Dog fight before, I didn't know that he had a few tricks of his own. As the tremendous form lunged for his throat, Boy Dog seemed to duck. With his mighty jaws he took a good, firm bite into the bulldog's tender, left foot. There he held on with a grip as tight as a mighty steel trap. The bulldog let out a distressful, lingering yelp and fell limp, unable to move. He lay there helpless in the dusty gravel. Seeing as how the bulldog was unable to do any more harm and evidently was in much pain, I hurried over to Boy Dog, reached down, took hold of his collar, and issued a command.

"That's enough, Boy. Let him go now."

The big bulldog got up and took off like a scared rabbit. I seriously doubt he ever picked a fight with Boy Dog again.

"You old rascal," I said to him. "That's a pretty good trick. Where in the world did you learn to fight like that? We won't say anything to Dollie about this, except I imagine she'll know what's gone on by the looks of you." In every fight that I observed him in after that, he always used the same method of biting squarely into a tender paw, thus paralyzing his victim.

Messenger Boy

Boy Dog began going to work with me in the fields. When I'd work my mules, Gin and Doll, he'd make each and every round that we did, except for the times when the sun would beat down so miserably hot. Then Boy Dog would rest at the end of the row in the shade.

In my pocket, I'd carry a pencil and paper. Boy

Dog was my messenger. If I needed a part, if there was any kind of trouble, or if I simply needed a drink of cool water, I'd tie a note to his collar and say, "Go to the house, Boy Dog. Go find Dollie."

Without hesitating, he'd go straight to the house and find my wife. If she happened to be inside, he would bark loudly, letting her know that he had a message. If she was outside in the garden, he'd trot up to her and stand beside her until she noticed the note tied to his collar.

"What've you got there, Boy?" she'd ask. He'd wag his tail and gently nudge against her, feeling proud of himself because there was nothing he'd rather do than please one of us.

Jim, the Dog-Killing Mule

My Papa had bought a new mule from a man up at Kennett, Arkansas. The big, gray mule was named Jim and he was a dog killer.

"Now, Son," he said to me. "If you want to keep your dog alive, you'd better not let him get around this mule! Why just last week when Jack was helping me head Jim from the pasture into the lot, Jim whirled and kicked him. If I hadn't been right there, he would have stomped him in the ground. The man I bought Jim from said that he would kill any dog that made a fuss with him." He said that he had killed a couple of dogs for him and had broken another down in his back, so that now that dog wasn't good for nothing.

I always tried to keep Boy Dog away from Jim, so

I would sneak away whenever I'd pay Papa a visit. One day Boy Dog followed me over. From the house, Papa and I could hear him barking. We ran to the barnyard lot, and there was Boy Dog in the lot with Jim. He was barking and chasing after him.

"Get out of there, Boy Dog!" I shouted. "He'll kill you!"

Caught up in the excitement, Boy Dog paid me no attention.

Jim turned and headed toward him. He lowered his head to charge. This is what he always did just before he knocked a dog down, stunning him, so that he could pound and stomp his victim into the earth.

Teeth and Nose

I watched as Boy Dog stood there without backing up. Just when he got within reaching distance, he lunged forward, catching the soft part of Jim's nose in the same powerful grip of teeth as he had caught the bulldog's paw. Once again he had found a sensitive body part and had used it to his advantage. Boy Dog held on tight, moving under the oncoming mule. Jim flipped over and lay on the ground motionless, unable to move. I thought the mule had broken his back, but in a minute he lumbered to his feet and shook himself off. The two of them just stood there looking at each other. From that day on, whenever Papa wanted to catch Jim, all we had to do was call on Boy Dog! Jim would give us not a minute's trouble!

"If that isn't the darndest thing," Papa would say.

"I've never seen a dog that can fight like that! He sure is a smart one."

"Yes, I'm finding out that he's quite a dog. We wouldn't take anything in the world for Boy Dog."

A Reflection

It wasn't unusual for us to learn things from the animals on the farm. But Boy Dog was something else. He didn't know that the odds seemed to be against him, so they didn't bother him. He just expected and looked for a way to win! Little did I know then how much I would need to remember Boy Dog's example in the years to come.

2

A Farmer Goes to War

Six years passed. Things couldn't have been better. The farm was beginning to pay for itself, and we had hopes of replacing our three-room bungalow with a new-style farm house. Boy Dog proved to be a constant, loving companion. The year was 1941 and with it came rumors of war and then the bombing of Pearl Harbor.

I was thirty years old at the time, with no dependents except for my wife, Dollie, and, of course, Boy Dog (whom the Army didn't count as one). Although thirty was considered old for an enlisted man, single boys and men without children were issued their notices first. This made me a number-one draft choice and shortly word came that my departure date would be on October 17, 1942.

Dollie, Papa, and Boy Dog took me to the train station at Blytheville. From there I would travel to Little Rock, the state capital, and then be assigned to an army base. I thought of how Mama would have been there to see me off, too; but she'd passed on from us years before.

I stepped onto the train. Boy Dog ran alongside trying to get a footing on the first step. I reached down and patted his head.

"So long, Boy. You stay and look after Dollie while I'm gone, you hear?" With those words I gave him a gentle push backwards.

Waving goodby, I fought hard to hold back the tears. Boy Dog didn't understand why he couldn't make this trip with me, nor did I understand at the time the dangers that lay ahead for me and the loneliness that lay ahead for my wife and him as they remained behind.

"Hello, World!"

On arriving in Little Rock, I took notice of a lot of other country boys who looked just like myself. You could tell by just looking that most of us had not even been out of our own back yards, much less out of the state of Arkansas! Some came from the two bigger cities of Little Rock and Pine Bluff, but the majority of us were from the small rural counties and towns of the bottomland or from the hill regions of the Ozark Mountains. We were unlearned and ignorant in the ways of the world. Not knowing a sergeant from a lieutenant, we saluted everyone we met.

From Little Rock I was sent to Camp Adair, Oregon, where the 96th Division was formed. I was assigned to Company F with Colonel Halloran as my regimental commander. The 96th was a mid-continent division. Many of the men were from Tennessee, Alabama, Mississippi, Oklahoma, Missouri, and Arkansas. Upon arrival at Camp Adair, I figured that I'd gone at least halfway around the world. Leastwise, it was by far the farthest I'd ever been from home.

Learning to Be Tougher

In July 1943, more officers and men began trickling into camp. On July 28, the Army Ground Forces team made their visit and set the stage for Activation Day in August. It was here that we received the word that the 96th was to be no fancy, "goodtime Charlie" outfit, but simply a hard-slugging infantry machine. Our work had been cut out for us and I still remember General Bradley's words as he spoke: "Our enemies will be tough. We must be tougher. We kill or we get killed!" The words kept going over and over in my mind.

The next two months were rugged, with little time for homesickness. Being so busy helped ease the pain. Soldiers were supposed to be able to shoot, so we spent long hours on the shooting range. There were hikes, hikes, and more hikes. We would walk day into night and, when we could no longer stay in formation as we should, we'd hold on to each other's packs and keep going. We were allowed to fall asleep on our packs for ten minutes, then it was up and start walking again.

Out of the 180 men in my company, there was only one other man, Charlie, who was as old as myself. He was a big, red-headed Irishman from Chicago, the toughest guy that ever wore shoe leather! He would drink a case of beer at night and then be kicking and raring to go the next morning.

In the next, crucial, thirteen weeks, the men were separated from the boys; that's what the army called it. Starting out as civilians, we were being transformed into soldiers. We were becoming a group of disciplined, fighting men.

On February 20, 1944, our basic training was completed. The men of the 96th were trained soldiers. Now it would be the job of the army to mold each unit of the division into a single-purpose team.

Dollie, a Welcome Surprise

With basic training behind me, I lay there on my bunk one day in my army fatigues, wondering about what the army would have in store for us next. Then my buddy Raymond came hurrying in. Raymond was also an Arkansas boy and, likewise, from my hometown.

"Get up out of there, boy," he said. "Our wives are in town and they're waiting for us down at the depot!"

"Not my wife. She's not there." I protested, knowing that Dollie would never come all the way out west without writing me first.

"Yes, they are," he persisted. "They've just come in and they're down there waiting on us. Now get your britches on and let's go."

"All right, but you'd better not be pulling my leg."

I quickly switched my clothes, putting on my freshly laundered suntans, and Raymond and I were off for the depot.

On the way, I thought of all the soldiers' wives who had been unable to find housing. And even if we could find her a place to stay, there would be endless, lonesome hours for Dollie alone. Perhaps even in a single room. Soldiers' wives by the thousands were knocking on doors looking for room and board. And what about the farm—who'd look after Gin, Doll, and Boy Dog?

Suddenly we were there and, as soon as I saw her, my fears and doubts all subsided. There was my little gal from Arkansas! I'd recognize her anywhere. For a moment, however, she didn't recognize me! I was dressed and looked just like all my comrades. My hair was shorter, I was thinner, and I no longer wore the mustache I'd always had before.

"Hon, what in the world are you doing way out here?"

"I didn't know I was coming," she began. "Lorrine came over one night and the next morning we were ready and on our way here."

"Now, don't worry," she said, "your papa is going to watch after the farm and mother is going to keep Boy Dog. Everything will be fine, you'll see."

Dollie always had a special way of looking on the bright side. Everything else seemed unimportant, and I was so very glad that she had come to be with me.

With the Lord's help and the aid of a Baptist minister there in town, we were able to find room and board. Dollie found work at Montgomery Ward Stores and, whenever I could get a pass on the weekends, I'd come into town to be with her. The days didn't drag by any more. I'd work each day with more zest, always looking forward to the time I'd be able to spend with her.

At April's end, our division said "So long" to Camp Adair and moved on to Fort Lewis, Washington, for more training. Dollie moved along with me, once again finding work and housing.

On Maneuvers

Busy training days followed. We soldiers labored day after day, night after night, to learn the art of working as a team.

In late June, our division was ordered to the Oregon Maneuvers. We learned of the disasters that could come from little mistakes, from being a few minutes late or from lighting a match in the dark. We learned to eat what we could and sleep where we could. We learned that necessities come before comforts, but, above all, we LEARNED.

From living out of barracks bags around the lumber town of Bend to the wooden barracks of Camp White, we continued our amphibious training. Here we learned how to debark from a ship and how to make a beachhead landing.

Shipping Out

At Camp Beal we drew our overseas equipment. Rumors were circulating that our division would be heading out for the Philippine Islands, but nothing was yet official. On July 26, 1944, once again I kissed

PC Reservation Receipt

Reservation Number: 0890
PC: Readers' Services 15
Date: 4/2/2009
Time: 4:10 PM
Length: 60 minutes
Wait: 15 minutes
Location:
Readers' Services - 1st Floor

ALLEN COUNTY PUBLIC LIBRARY
HAVE YOUR LIBRARY CARD AND MATERIAL READY

TELEPHONE RENEWAL
(DURING MAIN LIBRARY BUSINESS HOURS ONLY)
(260) 421-1240

WEBSITE RENEWAL
www.acpl.lib.in.us
↳ MY LIBRARY ACCOUNT
↳ RENEW MATERIALS

ALLEN COUNTY PUBLIC LIBRARY

my wife good-by and left out of San Francisco Bay—
destination unknown!

After forty-two days on board ship we found ourselves unloading on the shores of the Hawaiian Islands. However, this was no vacation trip. Here we
took our jungle training and more amphibious training, and I continued my training as first scout.

Dollie's Exciting News

By this time I had received my first letter from
Dollie, and with it came exciting news.

Dearest Husband,

I have thrilling, wonderful news. I am expecting
a baby and come late March you'll be a papa. I saw
Dr. Fox this week and he said that was what those
sick spells I'd been having were all about. I can't tell
you how happy I am and how much I wish you to
be here with me.

I fear for you greatly, and Boy Dog must, too, for
the other night after I had gone to bed he raised up
the most lonesome howl I've ever before heard. I've
never known him to howl and the sound was awe-
some, sending chills up and down my spine. He was
wet from the rain, but I let him come into the house
and from that night on he has slept on the floor by
my bed. When I cook for myself I also cook enough
for Boy Dog. He is so much company to me with
you being so far away.

I had to sell Gin and Doll and the cattle, as they
were getting too much for me to take care of with
the winter coming on. Gin didn't seem to mind, but

Doll really threw a fit, and I had to leave the window as the men loaded her.

Mama stays here with me part of the time. Don't worry about me; just take care of yourself and be thinking of a name for the baby. May God be with you.

Love,
Your wife,
Dollie

Just think—me a papa, finally! I read the letter over and over. I told everyone that I met about my good news and I prayed that God would let me live to see this child.

Combat and the Lord

Our first step into combat was on the island of Leyte, in the Philippines. From there we traveled to Guam and Mindoro and Mindanao, each time sustaining heavy losses. The days were filled with violent attacks and fright, and the nights with sleeplessness because of the crashing sounds of artillery.

It was here that I came to know the Lord in a truly personal way and only He sustained me. The words of Psalm 56:3, "What time I am afraid, I will trust in thee," were always with me.

Once I was sitting next to a tree for protection. The position seemed to be a good one, but I felt I should move, so I did. A moment later the tree was blown up. I will always feel the Lord took care of me then.

Our biggest push was on the island of Okinawa,

where we lost practically our whole division. We went in with 125 men and only 25 of us, 20 percent of our division, walked out alive.

The emotional strain was intense. I could tell my roommate was not acting right. He had broken under the strain. I took him to the lieutenant in charge, but the lieutenant would not listen to me and sent him back. Wanting to help, I offered to make my friend's bed so he could lie down. I was on my hands and knees with my back to him when, out of the corner of my eye, I caught a glimpse of my friend with a dagger coming down between my shoulder blades. In a split second, I grabbed the blanket, twirled, and caught my friend. I marched him back to the lieutenant. "Lieutenant, I told you this man was sick. Now this time do something with him!" That time he did.

So far, for what reasons I didn't know, God was still protecting me, and I was still beating the odds. However, I was escaping all that danger only to ship out for mainland Japan.

Headed for Japan

We left Okinawa on an L.T.C cargo ship headed for Japan proper. Not long after we boarded the ship, we ran into a terrible storm at sea. The storm grew so violent that the captain ordered all of us below. We were below the main deck, where the trucks, jeeps, and tanks were stored. With every crash of the waves, the ship would make a loud cracking sound. With the storm raging so, I said, "Boys, the next one's going to get us!"

We had weathered the storm for one day and one night. It was nearing dusk when the storm began to pass over us. We were back port-side when the captain's voice blowed out through the loudspeaker.

"Now hear this, now hear this: It is a fact that the emperor of Japan has surrendered to the United States."

Stunned, no one said a word. We all just looked at each other.

Once again the captain's voice rang out.

"Now hear this, now hear this: It is a fact that the emperor of Japan has surrendered to the United States." It was the 14th day of August, 1945.

The War Is Over

The captain's second announcement broke the silence. Whooping and hollering, laughing and crying—I've never to this day heard the likes. We were a bunch of grown men making more of a ruckus than a bunch of school boys winning their first tournament game. For the first time in a very long while, we were breathing sighs of relief and actually laughing again.

We stayed up the rest of the night talking. I talked about my new baby, a beautiful, little girl whom I'd named Georgia Ruth, Georgia after my mother and Ruth after Dollie's mother. Now Boy Dog would have someone else to look after. I talked of seeing Dollie, Papa, and Grandma Jones. We southern boys talked about the farms, and I thought of how beautiful Arkansas was and how much I wanted to be there that very instant.

After months and months in the war-torn islands of the Pacific, by the grace of God, we were actually going home! The war was over!

3

A Soldier Returns Home

Time seemed to drag by endlessly as we were delayed an additional three months before setting sail for America. The trip home was much shorter than the trip over, though. This time we didn't have to stop on our way making up convoys and organizing fleets. In ten days from the time we left Mindoro, land was sighted. It wasn't just any land, though, it was the shores of the United States of America. Heaven couldn't have looked sweeter!

America's Welcome

Big yachts and fancy sailboats met us out in the ocean, and escorted us into the harbor. Men and women dressed in white were holding flags and banners. Bands were playing, and choirs sang out "The Star-Spangled Banner" and "My Country 'Tis of Thee." We felt the gratitude that was being bestowed on us by the supporters at home. It was truly a heroes' welcome! I thought of Woodruff, Olen, and big

37

Charlie, and how very proud they would have been to have shared with us this moment of glory.

As we docked we could see thousands more waiting to greet us. We all ran dock-side, almost sending the enormous ship for a sideways tumble.

The captain's voice sounded over the loud speaker: "Attention! All personnel report below. In an orderly manner!"

As we stepped from the gang plank to American soil, the first thing we did was to kneel and kiss the ground, and I said "Thank You" to God in my heart! There were people lined up on each side waiting to shake hands with the men who'd helped win the war and had returned home.

The army had efficiently gathered information and had arranged for each soldier a five-minute telephone conversation with a member of his family. Since we had no telephone, I had sent word for Dollie to be at the central telephone office in our hometown of Leachville on the afternoon of December 21. We were taken to a large depot in San Francisco and ushered into a long hallway where telephone booths stood on each side for a distance of two hundred yards or more. As each soldier's call was placed, his name was spoken over an intercom. You could have heard a pin drop as everyone sat quietly awaiting his turn.

As my name was called and I walked to the booth, I kept going over all the important things I wanted to say. My hand trembled as I picked up the telephone. I managed to utter a single, "Hello," before my voice failed me. Dollie picked up the conversation on the other end, and I listened intently as she tried to hurriedly cover all the topics she knew I'd want to hear about. I heard my daughter jabber and I knew that she was saying "I love you, Daddy." It was nearing Christmas Day, but I knew that I'd never make it home by then.

In the meantime, the Army was going all-out to treat us. After each soldier had a chance to talk, we were taken to a large cafeteria in the same building and allowed to order anything. Being, oh, so hungry for some southern cooking, I ordered steak with white soup, beans, and cornbread.

Back to Arkansas

After three days in San Francisco, I found myself on a southern-bound train headed for Arkansas. I arrived in Little Rock and continued my journey on to Blytheville with a buddy of mine. As I stepped off the train, I thought of how this was the very spot where I'd said my farewells an eternity ago, it seemed to me.

I made my way to the outskirts of town. With my army pack on my back, I was going to try my luck at hitchhiking the remaining twenty miles.

As I stood there beside the edge of the highway, a car began slowing down to stop. The man inside rolled down the window and said, "Get in, soldier!" Then he looked over at me again. "Well, well, Ike, is that you?"

It was Mr. Kennett, a man I knew from Leachville. We shook hands and he tried to catch me up on all the news from home.

"You know, Ike," he said, "that big, red dog of yours has been seen all over this country! He's been seen in town and at practically all the neighbors' houses, especially when you and your wife were both gone. Looking for you all, I suppose. Everybody just seemed to watch out for him. I suppose the folks here at home thought they might be helping you out in the war, in some small way, by looking out for him. He'd stay somewhere a day or so and then move on. He's quite a dog."

"Yes, that he most certainly is," I replied. "Thanks for looking out for him and thanks for the ride," I said, as we approached the road that led from the highway to my house.

"Don't you want me to run you on down to your house?" he asked.

"If you don't mind, Mr. Kennett, I'd rather just walk from here. Thanks again for the ride. Good-bye."

It was the twenty-eighth day of December, 1945, and there was a chill in the morning air as I stepped out of his car and onto the dirt road—the dirt road that led home.

As I stood there buttoning up my overcoat, I looked toward my house and then over toward Papa's house. I wondered how he was feeling today. Dollie had said that he hadn't been feeling well lately. I looked at the stalks left standing there in Mr. Moore's cotton field and I wondered if he'd had a good crop this year.

I felt the anticipation growing inside as I picked up my bag and started walking, knowing that shortly I'd be seeing my daughter and my wife. This was the day I'd dreamed of, night after night, as I'd laid in the foxholes. I almost had to pinch myself to realize that I was no longer dreaming.

Boy Dog Remembers

A little over halfway, where the tall cottonwood stood, I could see the house in full view. I stopped and whistled, wondering if Boy Dog would hear. I watched as he raised his head in a curious manner from where he lay resting on the old meat block. At first he didn't move, but his ears were standing upright and he was watching me. I whistled again. This time he bounded off the front porch onto the frozen earth and here he came! He had remembered the whistle! He knew who I was!

I dropped my bag and knelt down on one knee as he came closer. "Here, Boy," I said, observing his actions closely. No human face could have shown more emotion than did Boy Dog's. As I put my arms around his mighty neck, I felt his old heart pounding heavily and I noticed the streaks of gray that were mingled in among the red. Boy Dog had become an old dog. The years had taken their toll and he had aged greatly in the four years that I'd been away.

"I'm home, fellow," I said. "You don't have to go out looking any more. I'm home to stay."

He barked as if to say he understood what I was saying.

"Now, Boy Dog, let's you and me get on toward the house. I've been looking forward to this day for a long time and, by the way, fellow, I think that you've got somebody to introduce me to, haven't you?"

A Reflection

The story above shows how, time after time, God did protect me and how, with Him, I did beat the odds. He was there. He did care.

A couple of years after I returned home, Boy Dog died. But by then I was blessed with a son. I wish I could have spared him some of the trials he would have to face, but then that wasn't God's way. I guess I should have known that God would have to lead my son through trials, too. It was all in His perfect plan.

PART TWO

Trials of the Second Generation
Frank Minirth, M.D.

4

A Young Man Fights for Life

Less than a year after Dad's return from the war, I was born. Life on the farm was good. It was hard for me, however, because I was small for my age. So early on just to keep up I had to develop a fighting attitude toward life.

I grew up in an extremely strong Christian family. My mother was very loving and shared Christ with me when I was a young boy. My father was a good example, too. Each year when he would take all of us boys in his Sunday school class on a campout, I would be extremely happy. I felt a sense of pride when I could say, "He's my father," for I knew that he was a man of integrity.

Then, the same year that I received Christ in my life, I was diagnosed as having diabetes mellitus. From then on, I had a new fight. I fought a fear of dying young, a fear of being different, the pain of taking shots every day, the fear of a chronic disease that I would never get over, the sadness that I could never eat all the delectable delights that tempt chil-

dren—pies, cakes, and other delicious foods. But the
fighting produced in me a self-discipline that has been
more and more valuable to me as life has gone on.

Three years after my diagnosis as diabetic, I came
close to dying. I caught pneumonia and my blood
sugar level shot up very high. I was in the hospital
a week. However, because I was a fighter, I was back
in school within two weeks.

I was always fighting to stay alive. I was in the
ninth grade, stood four feet, nine inches tall and
weighed ninety pounds. My parents, Ike and Dollie,
were very supportive during those teenage years and
encouraged me all they could. Of course, they also
were concerned about me.

Off to College

Partly because of my own medical problems and
the resulting contact with the field of medicine, I decided to become a medical doctor. I could see that
medicine offered a great avenue for ministry for the
Lord. I was interested in pursuing either the field of
general medicine, as a general practitioner, or the
field of psychiatry. Both offered ways to combine
physical, psychological, and spiritual healing. I
wanted to be involved in helping to heal people, as
well as to point them to the ultimate Healer, Jesus
Christ.

When I left the farm for college, Arkansas State
University at Jonesboro, thirty miles away, I had
grown to five feet, four inches, and weighed about

118 pounds. My diabetes was still a great concern and, frankly, life was rough.

During those early college years, a boy, in a sense, becomes a man. I realized this and also became aware that I must now make several tough and life-altering decisions on my own. As I faced these decisions, however, I felt an inner uneasiness. I longed to walk with the Lord; yet I was not close to Him, and I knew it. I was struggling physically and spiritually. And then a strange turn of events came into my life.

High on Christ

I was not able to withstand the physical problems college dormitory life presented, so I began to commute the thirty miles back and forth from home. A young minister from my local church, States Skipper, asked to commute with me. This was when drug abuse on campus was at a zenith and there was a lot of talk about the "highs" that drugs gave. States, however, seemed "high" on Christ. He would sing the old hymns of the faith. He would talk about Jesus. He knew Christ personally; Jesus seemed to be his best friend. States stressed only Christ and avoided any issues that might distract from Him.

Soon States and I heard of a Bible study on campus and decided to attend. The teacher enjoyed Bible verses like I enjoyed my favorite food. His eyes glistened as he talked about Christ. His voice would vibrate with excitement as he talked about the Lord. I was deeply impressed, but I must admit, I was skeptical.

Are they crazy? I thought. *They certainly are different. I've never seen people so excited about Christ. They actually seem "high" as they share Bible verses and talk about the Lord. Could a person be "high" on just Christ alone?* On and on the thoughts rambled through my head. And week after week, the members of the Bible study remained "high" on Christ.

Soon their enthusiasm for Christ and for life affected me. I began to fight back, physically and spiritually. If I was ever going to realize my dream of having an effect for Christ in my chosen field of psychiatry, I must fight—and fight now. I worked out physically. I refused to die young.

I caught some of my Bible teacher's enthusiasm. I had a long way to go, but I could feel the beginning of that closeness with the Lord. I could feel sure and certain emotions as I memorized:

> Be anxious for nothing.
>
> Peace I leave with you.
>
> Casting all your care upon him,
>   for he careth for you.
>
> I will never leave thee,
>   nor forsake thee.

My old black Bible became worn. I searched it day and night. Answers were coming. My destiny seemed to be clearer. Then life took another dramatic turn.

Left Out

I was not handsome; truthfully, I was homely. I seldom dated in high school since I was very small for my age. In fact, my girlfriend in high school was about a foot taller than I and outweighed me by nearly fifty pounds! Not that she was so large, I was just so small. God knew I had some misgivings about this, but it just seemed to be the way things were, so I felt I must accept it. Oh, not that I didn't fight back, but I had a long way to go, even with my weight lifting! Anyway, I was definitely not among the top three eligible men. In fact, I often identified with an old song that went as follows:

> God gave to the wise men their wisdom,
> To the poets he gave them their dreams,
> To father and mother their love for each other,
> But He left me out, though, it seemed.

I was still small when I was in college. However, at last I began to grow and consistent working out began to pay off a little. As an upper classman I was five feet, seven inches, and weighed all of 130 pounds! And I began to date more, girls my own size now.

Meeting Snow White

States often talked about a brunette journalism major that sat just behind him in class. Well, I couldn't help it, I had always been attracted to brunettes. One day at Baptist Student Union, there she sat. States had not introduced me. In fact, no one had told me Snow White's (that's how she appeared to me) name. I just knew that this must be the girl he had been talking about.

Would she go out with me? Might she even consider it? I probably don't have a chance.

And so the thoughts went.

The B.S.U. was having a Christmas carol sing, and a group of my friends went. Snow White happened to go, too. My heart thumped each time I glanced at her dark eyes. However, I was with my current girl friend.

I didn't have any psychological training then, but I did know what guilt felt like. What was I doing? I was with one girl, but thinking about another. My best friend had told me about the other girl, so he must be interested in her, too. I, however, (ashamed, as I ought to be to say so) fought off such rational thinking. The thought that threw off all others was, *Would she go out with me?*

Well, there was only one way to find out. I picked up the phone. My hands trembled as I dialed. The phone rang. "Hello," she said. My heart jumped. I valiantly fought the quiver in my voice as I tried to tell her who I was and to ask her for a date. Just as I expected, she said no. I knew it, I knew she wouldn't go! Well, while I had her on the phone, I might as well ask her if she would go out with me the next week. "Yes." Did she say yes? I almost fainted, but maintained my composure as I coolly told her that I would see her then.

More Than My Share

The date worked out fine. Again, I was struck with the fact that she too was "high" on Christ. She had a quiet and gentle spirit and was very different from any girl I had met. And, believe it or not, she seemed to like me! At last I could identify with the last verse of that song I used to sing, which, after we had dated awhile, I would often sing to her.

> God gave to the wise men their wisdom,
> To the poets He gave them their dreams,
> To father and mother, their love for each other,
> But He left me out, though, it seemed.
> I went around broken-hearted
> Thinking life was an empty affair.
> But when God gave me you,
> It was then that I knew
> He had given me more than my share.

After she heard my singing, I was surprised that Mary Alice ever consented to marry me; but she did!

A Reflection

When Mary Alice agreed to marry me, she said she had always prayed for someone who would be different, and I easily met that qualification. I wasn't sure how to take that. Later on she clarified that statement: not only had she thought me courageous in my fight with diabetes, but I also was deeply committed to the Lord and was seeking to find His will for my life. Had we met before I became involved with that Bible study, however, I wonder if she would have been as interested in me. I felt my finding a wife like Mary Alice, when I did, was truly beating the odds.

5

Taking the Less-Traveled Road

My roughest challenge lay ahead—medical school. I had always been at the top of my class, but this time I met my match. The courses were unbelievably hard! The students were unbelievably smart!

I would study late into the night. I would study at the supper table. I would study on Friday night, all day Saturday, and all day Sunday. The long, long hours of study zapped my energy. My weight dropped from 130 to 120 pounds. I was working out every day with weights, trying to increase my stamina, as well as my size. Still, I continually felt exhausted. The diabetes fought back and I struggled with it. "I must get up just one more day," I would tell myself morning after morning. I felt discouraged and wondered if I would ever be able to make it through medical school.

But God's sovereignty intervened once again.

Meeting Over a Cadaver

I was taking a cadaver class, which was far from my favorite course in medical school. Then I discovered that my cadaver mate—the student assigned to study dead bodies with me—was also a Christian. But he wasn't just any Christian! He shared how he had given his life to the Lord to use in medicine. He wanted to have an effect for Christ. Several elderly, godly saints had been praying for him for years, he said, and he must not disappoint them. And even more important, he must not disappoint Christ. He had a destiny he must find. He too was "high" on Christ.

During those rough days in medical school, we became mutual encouragers. We became close Christian friends. Together we would sit down and ask ourselves how we could have an effect for Christ in our lifetime. That friend was Paul Meier.

Balancing Scripture and Psychiatry

Later on, as Paul began a psychiatry residency and I was on a rotating internship in general medicine and psychiatry, we carefully weighed everything we were learning on the scales of Scripture.

Although many people considered psychiatry a field that wasn't compatible with Christianity, Paul and I decided that, using a strong scriptural background as a grid, we could determine which areas of psychiatry fell within scriptural guidelines and which did not. While we both had strong biblical and theological backgrounds before medical school (to which we have added substantially since our medical school days), at times we checked out questionable areas of our studies with theologians more qualified than ourselves. We still continue that practice today. We were

fortunate, too, that a number of our psychiatry pro-
fessors were Christians who encouraged us in this
practice.

As a result, we became aware of the truth behind
the scientific findings of psychiatric experiments and
studies which secular psychiatrists would often mis-
interpret when making their conclusions. The truth
of 1 Corinthians 2:14 (NIV) was evident to us as we
studied. "The man without the Spirit does not accept
the things that come from the Spirit of God, for they
are foolishness to him, and he cannot understand
them, because they are spiritually discerned."

Of course, we realized that not only the Spirit of
God in our lives was needed as we studied psychiatry, but the Word of God also. We found that many
psychiatric findings which agreed with Scripture's
outlook on human behavior were just good "common" scriptural sense. Most Christians with a strong
scriptural background and a healthy Christian outlook on life, if given the scientific findings of psychiatry, could see which psychiatric conclusions were
scriptural and true, and which were not.

A Fork in the Road

Following my rotating internship, I was still de-
bating which way to go, into general practice or psychiatry. Then an opening for a straight psychiatry
residency became available. I took it, even though
my interest in general medicine was just as strong
(and continues to be to this day) as my interest in
psychiatry. I now realize, of course, that that psy-

chiatry residency opening—God's opening—was a major fork in the road.

I became Chief Resident in Psychiatry at the University of Arkansas Medical Center. This led to an invitation from Dallas Theological Seminary to teach pastoral counseling, thereby also giving me the opportunity to start a psychiatric practice in Dallas.

Since that time, my friends Paul Meier and States Skipper, as well as many other well-trained and accredited Christian counselors—psychiatrists, psychologists, and therapists—have joined me. The ministry God has given us over the years is a testimony to the grace of God.

A Reflection

God always seemed to intervene in my life when the odds against me seemed bad indeed.

My decision to accept Christ as my Savior the same year that I was diagnosed a diabetic.

My meeting so many Christians, including States, who were "high" on Christ, at a time when I realized I couldn't face alone the challenges that college life presented.

Finding Mary Alice, who was "more than my share," after we both had discovered what it was to be "high" on Christ. That shared spiritual "high" helped to give me the edge among the many boys interested in her. It brought together two people who were otherwise at opposite ends of the "dating pole."

Meeting Paul Meier at a time when I needed the encouragement of another Christian medical student.

The psychiatric residency opening that helped me choose my destiny when I didn't know which way to go.

Of course, I know that God was guiding all along, not just in those trying times. Like many people, however, I seemed to recognize His intervention only when it was apparent, from the human perspective, that I could no longer beat the odds on my own.

PART THREE

Trials of the
Third Generation
Mary Alice Minirth

6

The Threat of Losing a Family

When I accepted Christ at the age of nine, I knew exactly what I was doing. The gospel was very clear. I knew that I was human and therefore imperfect and sinful, and that I needed God's plan for salvation and eternal life.

But what happens during the time between our initial belief in Christ and the time we are made into His likeness in heaven? Some Christians give the impression that this time will be all rosy. But the Bible does not promise an easy, uncomplicated life.

As I grew in the Lord, I also felt that He would have me do something special for Him. I listened attentively to missionary stories at vacation Bible school and I saw God working through the committed lives of Christians around me. These people were my heroes. But how does one develop faith and commitment like these people?

The Chosen Path

I had made a choice for Christ. I was committed to Him and felt He had a special plan for my life.

61

Following the "straight and narrow high road" wasn't a hard choice for me, even during my teenage years. I knew Christians were expected to be different. It was lonely sometimes, but I didn't think of it as suffering.

There were two things that I asked God for during my teenage days as a Christian. One, I hoped to do something special for Him (possibly in the field of Christian journalism) and, second, I really wanted to do that something special with a committed Christian husband.

I entered college with a small journalism scholarship and a lot of zeal. I met the man of my dreams three months later. Frank was also a committed Christian looking for God's plan for his life.

Frank and I were committed to God and committed to each other. So we lived happily ever after, right? That is almost true. We claimed the verse in Philippians that states ". . . he which hath begun a good work in you will perform it until the day of Jesus Christ" (Phil. 1:7, KJV). God did start a work in us individually and as a couple, and He is not finished yet.

Frank had suffered for years with diabetes. He showed great courage and commitment, however, so I didn't worry about his health. I also brought a lot of commitment and zeal to our marriage.

Busy for the Lord

When Frank entered medical school, he had to study night and day. I was also studying, to make it through my last two years of college. And I held a part-time job. For practical reasons, I replaced a journalism career with a career in education. Frank and I had no time for anything but work.

So between work and work, we worked! Work wasn't suffering, because we were goal-oriented, anyway. We had God, His plans for us, and our love for each other.

During the summer of our third year of marriage our schedules eased a bit. I had worked a year as a teacher and we actually had some income. We spent the summer helping with my sister's wedding preparations, spending five weeks at a training center for Christian discipleship, and traveling through Colorado and California.

Troubles Appear

Then my Dad was diagnosed with malignant lymphoma (a cancer of the lymph glands), and for six weeks, off and on, I had menstrual troubles. The first day I returned to teaching, the pains became so severe that I finally decided to go to the doctor. He told me that I was suffering from a miscarriage! I had not realized I was pregnant; I just thought I had an irregularity problem.

Within a short time my blissful outlook on life changed drastically. Here I was, a committed Christian, wanting to do God's will. My Dad had cancer, my husband had diabetes, and I had had a miscarriage. To me, it seemed as if my past, present, and future were all being wiped out! My dad, on whom

I could always depend, might die; my husband, who had diabetes could die; and I might never have children!

My commitment to Christ did help me through this first miscarriage. But when I suffered a second miscarriage and then a third, all within a two-year period, my faith was really shaken. For someone who had never had even a tooth cavity, these miscarriages were devastating. Every medical book said that, with each miscarriage, the chances of carrying a child to term become less. Reading this over and over, I felt hopeless. I asked, "God how am I supposed to have faith when my past, present, and future show no promise?"

Thwarted at Every Turn

A very godly lady encouraged me by telling me how she could see me being used to bring other people to Christ. *Well, if I can't be a mother physically,* I thought, *I can still be a spiritual mother. I can tell people about Christ and study the Bible with them.* A short time later, a couple with whom we had been spending time in Bible study decided that God and Christianity weren't for them and they took a different path in life.

Again, I felt hopeless about my past, present, and future. I was almost clinically depressed. I wanted to sleep a lot, and I couldn't even express myself in a Sunday school class.

Why, I wondered, *would God let someone who was committed to Him go through all this? Why would*

He yank the rug out from under my past, present, and future?

God's "Big Picture"

Why, indeed! I now feel that God needed to review with me the "big picture," His overall plan for my life to glorify Him. According to Psalm 139, my past, present, and future were planned before I was born. "All the days ordained for me were written in your book before one of them came to be" (NIV). I meditated on this verse and I also claimed the promise that He wouldn't give me more than I could bear.

Frank felt as sad as I did about not having children, but somehow he never lost hope. I think his hope came from his mother who was childless for ten years before giving birth to Frank's sister and then Frank.

Leaning on Another's Hope

Frank knew how sad and depressed I was. One day he sat me down and said that, with God's help, we would have a child. We would do everything we could, he said, and then we would leave the rest up to God. I, however, did not have enough faith to try once more. I was afraid of failing again.

I had been going to Bible study, however, and God had shown me lots of examples of faith in the Scriptures. Still, at times, I felt like Sarah when she laughed inside the tent at the angels who told Abraham that she and Abraham would have a child.

Encouraged by Scripture and Frank's confidence, I became pregnant a fourth time. We decided that I would spend the first three months resting completely. We had a Christian doctor who had faith, too. Any other doctor would have told us to forget any plans for a child, because the odds were against us.

Sitting and Waiting

Our plan was for me to stay in the house and to rest for the whole nine months, if necessary. The days went by slowly! Then, finally, we were able to hear the heartbeat. The baby was alive! We got past three months, four months—the times when I had previously miscarried. At five months, I actually had to wear maternity clothes.

Frank brought home boxes of food for me. I didn't lift a finger but concentrated on reading Scripture and organizing our life the best I could while sitting down. Things were going fine until I reached my thirty-second week of pregnancy. The doctor said that I was showing signs of premature labor. That was a shock! How could that happen after thirty-two weeks of doing nothing but lying down?

Lying in Wait

I spent six weeks in the hospital lying flat on my back. We felt that this was better than risking the baby's premature birth and having to place it in an incubator. It was a frightening time, because I imagined that every little pain would lead to stronger labor pains and to a premature baby. And, all along, I feared that the baby would not be healthy. After six weeks, the labor pains seemed to stop. The doctors sent me home to wait, since the baby would now be sufficiently developed for healthy survival.

I went home and waited, living on an emotional roller coaster! After trying for eight-and-a-half months to keep the baby from being born too early, the baby decided to wait awhile.

A Baby Beats the Odds

Two weeks later the labor pains returned and were close enough together that the doctor decided I should return to the hospital. On December 13, 1974, after two hours of labor, Rachel Marie Minirth was born. She was a healthy, bright-eyed, 7-pound, 11-ounce girl. Her dad and I were ecstatic.

Frank and I had been married seven years. The Lord had continued His plan for our lives in his own way and with His own timing. We named her from the verse in Genesis that says, "And Jacob served seven years for Rachel; and it seemed unto him but a few days, for the love he had to her" (Gen. 29:20, KJV).

Rachel had to spend ten days in the hospital because of jaundice, a temporary liver condition in newborns, but she came home on December 23 to help us celebrate the happiest Christmas of our lives.

A Reflection

Since then, God has shown me many times that,

in marriage, one partner often has extra faith when the other one has less. I don't think that this is necessarily a sign of weakness, but God's plan for balance in a marriage.

7

New Beginnings

When Rachel was four months old, we moved to Dallas, Texas, so that Frank could teach at Dallas Theological Seminary and set up a Christian psychiatric practice. That year, 1975, was a year marked by changes—a new family, a new ministry, a new location.

Sometimes we felt lonely and we missed our families. But we had just seen a great miracle worked in our lives and God, we believed firmly, would continue to lead us.

A few years prior to our move, we had attended a Christian Medical Society retreat at Pine Cove Conference Center in East Texas. It was there that we first met Haddon Robinson, president of the Christian Medical Society, and Phil Hook, both of whom were teaching at Dallas Theological Seminary. They could see the need for instructors with our backgrounds to teach pastoral counseling at the seminary.

Most of the people there, however, qualified doctors and medical students alike, were surprised that Frank (and Paul Meier, who was there with his wife,

Jan) had chosen psychiatry as a field of Christian ministry. We were told many times that most Christians they knew who had chosen to go into psychology, much less psychiatry, had lost their faith! For Paul and Frank, however, Scripture was to be the base of all they were learning, practicing, and hoped to be teaching.

God's Leading to Dallas

Frank and Paul had already visited other cities with the idea of establishing a practice together, but God kept introducing Frank and me to people from the Dallas area. Soon we met Don Meredith, head of Christian Family Life, and Gene Getz, another Dallas seminary professor, who pastored the church Don had helped to start. They encouraged us to come to Dallas to teach and to establish a psychiatric practice.

So here we were in the spring of 1975 in Dallas, Texas, temporarily living with Don and Sally Meredith and their children, while Frank tried out teaching as a team teacher with Gene Getz in an alumnae refresher course for established pastors.

The textbook Frank used was *Christian Psychiatry*, the book he spent much of his residency writing. At that time many people felt that when it came to Christianity and psychiatry "never the twain should meet!" These returned seminary alumnae, however, were very open to what Frank was teaching. With their experiences in pastoral counseling, they could see the need for using psychological and psychiatric knowledge in Christian counseling. (We later found that inexperienced seminary students sometimes had a harder time seeing how psychology and psychiatry could be used in Christian counseling.)

Not long after we moved to Dallas, the Merediths moved. So, here we were, in a strange location, trying to start a ministry, settle down, and make friends. Frank probably felt most alone that year. There were no other psychiatrists around him practicing from a Christian perspective.

With one car, in a city with little public transportation, Rachel and I would take Frank to the clinic early to see his 7:30 A.M. appointments before he started teaching at the seminary that day.

Three Generations Continue

Three years later, I had a fourth miscarriage. When a sixth pregnancy occurred, however, we received much help in our home from our parents and from Christian friends. All of them helped in their way to give us our second daughter, Renee Ruth Minirth, who was born August 26, 1978.

When my parents arrived at the hospital, Dad shared with us that, just a few days earlier, his doctor had told him (after eight years of chemotherapy) that his cancer was cured. I lay in the hospital bed praising my God!

The Clinic Expands

During our second year in Dallas we were joined by Paul Meier and his family and thus the Minirth-

Meier Clinic was established. Within another year, three more people—a psychiatrist and two psychologists—joined us. One colleague was States Skipper, Frank's commuting friend from his early years in college, who was now a pastor turned psychologist.

The opportunity to teach pastors and seminary students preventative therapy was the primary reason for our move to Dallas. We never envisioned the growth of the clinic to what it is today and promises to become in the future. And the clinic's peripheral ministries, books and media, could well help many more people than the clinic will firsthand.

Two Are Better Than One

The real plus of the clinic, for Frank and the others working there, is to have so many people with whom they can talk things over, from a Christian standpoint. Each person brings a rich variety of knowledge and wisdom to the different problems the counselors face. In setting up the clinic, Frank claimed the verse:

> Two are better than one,
>   because they have a good return for their work:
> If one falls down,
>   his friend can help him up.
> But pity the man who falls
>   and has no one to help him up!
>
> Ecclesiastes 4:9–10, NIV

In 1981, two important things happened. First, we were blessed with another little girl, Carrie Rebecca.

Next, Frank and Paul saw their book, *Happiness Is A Choice,* published by Baker Book House. That popular book, on the symptoms, causes, and cures of depression, introduced the clinic to the Christian world at large. People from all over the country started coming to the clinic for further help.

Ten years after it was started, the Minirth-Meier Clinic had branch clinics in several cities and a staff of fifty psychiatrists, psychologists, and therapists—all committed Christians. Patients come from all over the United States; some are treated on an out-patient basis in the clinic; others are admitted to one of the psychiatric hospital wards that the clinic staffs.

Today Frank enjoys all phases of his ministry. He does a variety of things: teaching, counseling, performing medical diagnoses, prescribing medicines, appearing on radio and TV programs, speaking in churches and for community groups and preparing audio-visual materials.

The Need for Counseling

I often think that the need for Christian counseling clinics has arisen because many Christians come from non-Christian or less than healthy Christian environments. With the Judeo-Christian culture a thing of the past, and families uprooted from childhood friends, churches, and loved ones, people find themselves alone when it comes to seeking help in living their lives. The ideal and biblical way to meet problems is, first, through the family, then through the church. But in today's mobile society, people don't know each other well enough to call on those around them for help. And it is difficult to know who around us really needs help. The Christian counseling center becomes the answer.

Our lives today are very different from our first days in Dallas. It is not at all unusual, when we are in public, to have people come up and tell Frank what his ministry or the ministry of other clinic members has meant to them or to their family members. We often have former patients call in to the clinic's television or radio talk-show programs and say how well they are now doing.

Of course, occasionally we meet someone who hasn't been too happy with the therapy he or she has received. Frank keeps learning, as do the others on the staff. But the patients themselves must be willing to do all they can to achieve a happy, balanced life.

I see Frank's ministry as Christian medical pioneering. There have been other fields of medicine that, at one time, were looked on askance by some Christians, but which today have many Christians practicing successfully, Christians who have probably made those fields better because of the input of their Christian viewpoints. Certainly, we feel that this is becoming true with Christian psychiatry.

We feel we have beaten the odds, in our family and in Frank's ministry. But we know that, on down the road, other odds will appear to be against us, until we look to God's guidance and strength to overcome them.

A Reflection

Writing these chapters is a fulfillment of the dream I had years ago. I wanted to do something in Christian journalism. I had the skill, but I didn't have a message. God's grace and guidance in overcoming my trials has now given me a message.

When people today ask me how I have patience in different areas, I tell them that I have had practice building up patience. My trials and everyday living have helped me to look at the big picture with God's help. God has blessed in many ways, but realizing that only three things are eternal (God, His Word, and the lives of people) really puts life in perspective. Common household troubles—frozen pipes that have burst or items stolen from our home—are only minor irritations compared with the working out of God's big picture. The big picture is His plan to bring us to Himself and to work in us to His glory.

We do not let a week go by without telling our children what God has done for us.

PART FOUR

Helps to Overcome Life's Trials

Frank Minirth

8

The Whys and Wherefores of Suffering

So often I hear the question, "Why do people, especially Christians, suffer?" And, all too often, the questioner says that he or she has never been given anything but a bewildered look as a reply to that question. God, however, does have an answer to that question; in fact, many answers. The answer that usually comes to the minds of most Christians (but which they don't like to give for fear of offending the one who is suffering) is, "Because of sin." Certainly, sin is a reason for *some* suffering, but it is not always the reason.

I found in the Book of Job a reason for suffering that would not easily be determined just from human logic. This book of the Old Testament first became meaningful to me in college. I suppose I became interested in Job's sufferings because of my own diabetes and resulting lack of stamina.

Before I studied Job's experiences, I used to try to bargain with God to cure my diabetes. And I spent many an hour trying to figure out why I had it. Finally, however, I gave all that up and decided not only to cope with diabetes, but also to see what good could come out of it. As it says in Romans 8:28 (KJV) "All things work *together* for good for those who love God and who are the called according to His purpose" (italics added).

First, I realized that if I had never had diabetes, I probably would not have developed an interest in the field of medicine. More than likely I would have followed my dad into farming in Arkansas, a much-needed profession, but one that would have given me little opportunity to affect the lives of people as directly as the field of psychiatry.

Second, to survive, a diabetic must lead a disciplined life regarding diet, meal times, exercise, and rest. Without the diabetes, I realized, I would not have developed the self-discipline that has been beneficial to me in areas other than just my personal health. The success of my practice has been this disciplined lifestyle that is now second nature to me. (I do alter my schedule when family or other needs call for change. But living and working in a disciplined manner is not a problem for me.)

The Cart Before the Horse

A reason for trials and suffering that many people, including Christians, often fail to consider is dramatized in the prologue (chapters one and two) of the Book of Job. Job's suffering is not the result of sin. Instead, such suffering might be considered a *forerunner* to *potential* sin. Satan wants to tempt believers to sin—to renounce God, His power or judgment, or both. So, with God's permission, Satan brings trials our way.

From another viewpoint, such permitted suffering is also a show of God's confidence in the strong faith of the believing sufferer not to sin but to keep on trusting Him. Such trust, God knows, would be not only a testimony to our world but also to the spiritual world of angelic beings, good and evil. We are little aware of that possibility.

War in the Heavenlies

We forget that there is an on-going war between Satan and God, between the forces of evil and the forces of good, going on "in the heavenlies," in the spiritual realm, that affects us here on earth. Until the Final Judgment that the Bible speaks about, Satan is allowed to rebel against God and to try to get others to join the rebellion. Satan wanted the moral, godly Job to rebel against God.

Job was a wealthy man, besides being moral and godly. He was "the greatest of all the men of the east" (Job 1:3) So Satan challenged God regarding Job's dedication, attributing it only to the many children and much material wealth God had given him. As a result, God gave Satan permission to rob Job of his ten children and his wealth, for God had confidence that Job's dedication to Him was not dependent on receiving good things from Him.

Right Reasons vs. Right Response

The main purpose of the Book of Job, however, is not, as we would first assume from this prologue—to show why the godly suffer. In fact, while this interchange between God and Satan regarding Job is revealed to the reader of the book, it was not revealed to Job, either before, during, or after his ordeal! Evidently, God never felt it necessary or wise to reveal the reason for Job's suffering to Job himself.

When Job lost his ten children and his wealth, he showed great spiritual strength. We are told,

> At this, Job got up and tore his robe and shaved his head [a sign of mourning]. Then he fell to the ground in worship and said:
> "Naked I came from my mother's womb,
> and naked I will depart.
> The Lord gave and the Lord has taken away;
> may the name of the Lord be praised."
>
> Job 1:20–21, NIV

or, as we more often hear it,

> "The Lord giveth and the Lord taketh away;
> Blessed be the name of the Lord."
>
> KJV

The book goes on to say that:

> In all this, Job did not sin by charging God with wrongdoing.
>
> Job 1:22, NIV

The primary lesson I learned from Job then is not the reason for a godly person's suffering but his or her *response* to suffering.

Sometime after this episode, Satan, still determined to break Job's dedication to God, challenged God again that loss of health and fear of death would surely turn Job against God. Still sure of Job's faith, God allowed Satan to take Job's health, but not his life (Job 2:6). As a result, Job then contracted a painful skin disease that covered his entire body.

Well-Meaning Friends, Bad Advice

With the disease, the plot thickens. Job's wife and friends offer their answers as to why men suffer. His distraught wife gives what might seem to be a logical explanation from viewing the observable evidence— *God is unfair* and unworthy of worship. She asks Job why he doesn't just "Curse God and die!" Job answers her by saying, "Shall we accept good from God, and not trouble?" (Job 2:9, 10, NIV).

Then Job's friends come and stay seven days with him before speaking to him. After this time, Job breaks his silence. Out of great physical and mental anguish, he says, in essence, "I wish I had never been born" (Job 3).

Shocked at Job's negative outlook, his friends feel compelled to give him advice. (It would have been better if they had continued their initial course of being present but silent.) Three of them offer the view of suffering that was widely accepted then and now— suffering is due to sin. They accuse Job, who contin-

ues to maintain his righteousness, of being a secret
sinner and hypocrite. (They could not accuse him of
outward or public sin, for his public actions and image were spotless.)

All Job needs to do, they insist, is acknowledge and
repent of his sin and God will lift these trials from
him. They dogmatically portray God as being spite-
ful and inflexible in His relations with mankind. Job,
however, keeps insisting that sin could not be the
reason, for he has been righteous in all his dealings,
both private and public.

The fourth friend, Elihu, younger but seemingly
wiser, waited until this long argument (twenty-seven
chapters worth!) ends in a stalemate. Then he gives
his own thoughts, which include (1) a view of sin
deeper than that which appears in the speeches of
his friends, (2) a profound atmosphere of reverence
for God, and (3) a picture of God who is not so much
a judge as He is a teacher.

> God is exalted in his power. Who is a teacher like
> him? Who has prescribed his ways for him, or said
> to him, "You have done wrong"?
>
>   Job 36:22, NIV

Elihu feels that suffering is a means of *purifying the
righteous and bringing them to a place of greater trust
in God*. While Elihu shows some wisdom in this, he
also lacks more comprehensive wisdom. Here, and
with other viewpoints he presents, he is too simplis-
tic in their application.

Knowing God Upstages Searching for Reasons

After Elihu finishes, God finally comes on the scene and interrupts all these long-winded speeches. Instead of revealing the reason for Job's trials—Satan's desire to get Job to rebel against God and God's own confidence in Job that he would not do so—God only assures Job that He was not acting in a haphazard way but according to consistent, intelligent design.

Then, instead of explaining what that design is, He takes Job on a mental tour of the universe and of the animal kingdom, asking Job if he knows how all these things were created and if he can create or rule them himself. As the awesomeness of God is revealed to him directly, Job's attitude toward his suffering is changed from hostility to humility and trust in an all-knowing, all-loving and all-powerful God, One whose greatness exceeds Job's ability to comprehend. Job is convinced that he can trust such a God completely.

He realizes that what had been, and still is, a puzzle to him is no puzzle to God. God did not answer the whys—the problems of his intellect. God did answer the problems of his heart—his spirit and his emotions. He heals Job's heart and quiet resignation and submission flood in. Job realizes that all is well with the world because God cannot fail.

The ways of God, Job now understands, are beyond us. God's knowledge and intellectual abilities, his intelligence quotient or I.Q., are far beyond ours. Ours are finite; His are infinite. There are mysteries beyond human comprehension.

When Job comes to know God, he no longer has to know why God allowed his trials. Job trusts God to do whatever is best. Truly, he has a change of heart and mind, a transformation of spirit, emotions, and intellect.

In the end, God does arrange for Job to overcome his trials. His health and many friendships are restored, he acquires new property, and he has more children. However, his original children, whom he loved and cared for so much were not returned.

Knowing Reasons Isn't Necessary

So this is what I learned from Job. I had been able to figure out some good that had come from my trials with diabetes—my entry into medicine and my learning a disciplined lifestyle. Whether or not I ever knew the primary purpose for my trials—my diabetes, small stature, dyslexia, and speech problems—didn't matter so much. Knowing that God's overwhelming love, power, and wisdom had all this under control was all I needed to submit willingly to coping with and trying to overcome my trials with the tools He made available to me. If God removed the diabetes, that would be great. If He didn't, then I trusted His greater intelligence and judgment. Truly,

My thoughts are not your thoughts, neither are your ways my ways, declares the Lord. As the heavens are higher than the earth, so are my ways higher than your ways and my thoughts than your thoughts.

Isaiah 55:8, 9, NIV

Principles of Overcoming

The Book of Job presents a number of principles that helped me as I sought to overcome life's trials, ones that, I believe, can help you too as you seek to live through and overcome your trials.

1. Remember that God is still in control. His power to keep the universe in control, including that part of it that is your little world, is without limits.

2. Realize that God's ways are above your ways. His knowledge and intellectual abilities work on a far higher plane than does your limited intelligence. Trying to figure out the reason or reasons for your trials may not be the best use of your efforts.

3. Learn to depend on God to overcome or live through trials. This helps you to know Him better. The more you come to know Him, the less important becomes any reason for your suffering that you could possibly understand.

4. Look at your attitude toward God and toward your trials and, if it needs changing, do so.

It may seem unlikely, but the story of Job's suffering, considered to be the oldest narrative in the Bible, is as relevant to overcoming your trials today as any you'll ever find.

9

How to Beat the Odds

What have the Minirths learned in overcoming trials that can be helpful to others? How did we beat the odds? There are nine responses that have proven especially helpful to us.

Realize that wrong responses will bring on more suffering

Trying to ignore our trials or repress the effect they are having on us will bring about:

Physical stress that will result in more physical suffering—ulcers, digestive disorders, heart strain or attacks, arthritis, or a milieu of other physical problems. The majority of hospital patients today have physical ailments that were caused or aggravated by wrong mental and spiritual responses to life's stresses.

Mental stress that is likely to result in clinical anxiety or depression (which often brings on physical ailments, as well).

Spiritual stress that will result in irresponsible behavior, including the choosing of inadequate ways of relief, such as alcohol or drugs, or venting anger (recognized or hidden) on other people.

As much as possible and as soon as possible, it has been helpful for me to remind myself of the eternal perspective. When I see my fleeting life as just a stepping-stone into eternity, what is happening here and now begins to take on less significance.

Of course, what eternity means to us affects how we will view the here and now. For instance, if eternity means living with the one who is the source of love itself, who loves us totally and perfectly, more than any person ever could, then the trials of these seventy-plus years on earth are much more bearable.

This promise of existence in a perfect eternity, of course, is available only to those who have accepted Jesus Christ as Savior and Lord. We may spend an eternity in heaven simply by trusting Jesus Christ, God's Son, and accepting that He personally died for each one of us, to pay for our sins. In other words, He took our place.

God is a loving God but He is also a just God. He cannot tolerate sin, and we are guilty of sin. If we were in a court room, the verdict would be guilty. The sentence would be an eternity spent in hell, completely devoid of anything that is godly and loving. By acknowledging our sinfulness and accepting—trusting in—Jesus' death on the cross as payment for our sins, we open the way for Jesus to take over our lives and through the Holy Spirit to mold us into the type of persons God meant us to be.

An anonymous hymn writer said:

He died for me on the mountain,
For me they pierced His side,
For me He opened that fountain,
The crimson, cleansing tide;
For me He waiteth in glory,
Seated on His throne;
He promised never to leave me,
Never to leave me alone.

This biblical perspective helps us to tolerate the trials that we are experiencing and helps to prepare us for accepting the fact that, eventually, we will face death. My dad survived a war, but age will inevitably overcome him. I may be healthy and strong at the present time, but eventually diabetes or another disease will take its toll. However, in the light of spending eternity in God's heaven, the threat of physical death takes on an entirely different significance.

Take action

Sometimes the cause of suffering and trials is apparent and a plan can be implemented to resolve the problem. I recall a young wife who came to see me. She was very upset over her husband's actions. She began to implement a plan: (1) Ask her husband to get professional counseling; (2) Ask herself how she could improve the marriage; (3) Work on their relationship; (4) Forgive her husband. If the cause can be found for the suffering, then often a plan can be implemented to overcome the trial.

I have found it very important in working with individuals to have them form a highly specific plan.

For example, an extremely upset young man came to see me. He had been living an immoral life. His new plan included: (1) Spending no time with his immoral friends or even going near their hangouts for one week. (Of course, at his next week's appointment, I would ask him to extend this commitment.) (2) Beginning a weekly personal Bible study. (I will often have individuals memorize each week one to three verses that deal with their specific problem area.) (3) Going to church on a regular basis and building some healthy friendships, always avoiding any activity in those relationships for which he might feel guilty (Prov. 4:15); (4) Beginning a regular exercise program (i.e., exercise every Monday, Wednesday, and Friday for thirty minutes from 7:30 to 8:00 A.M.).

Not only can we take action against spiritual and psychological problems, but often we can also take action against physical problems and resulting trials. For example, (1) Have a physical exam and talk with a doctor; (2) Take the medication that the doctor prescribes; (3) Exercise within our health limits; (4) Maintain a positive outlook. Realize that new medicines and medical procedures are increasing at an unbelievable rate. There is hope. I went from a four-foot, nine-inch, ninety-pound weakling in the ninth grade, to an average-sized person simply through hard work—day after day of weight training, exercise, and refusing to give up.

During my sophomore year of medical school I recall reading in a textbook a statement something to this effect: "All too often, the course of diabetes is swift and downhill. In the early twenties, the person just dies." At that time I already had the "sophomore syndrome" (a sophomore medical student thinks he has every disease he studies and will probably die the very next day), and that statement shook me up. The next day at 5:00 A.M. I was out jogging. I was ready to fight back!

Also at that time, I took speech lessons. I couldn't speak plainly as a small child and wanted to overcome that problem. (Of course, I still have more than a slight Southern accent!) As a child I had an oddly-shaped head. Unfortunately there were no exercises to correct that; but physical maturity eventually helped to alleviate that problem.

Furthermore, I suffered from a form of dyslexia (a reading impairment). So I had to work hard in school, especially in spelling, because my brain interpreted letters of words in a different order than they actually occurred. As a result, I often studied late into the night.

In other words, fight back. Don't give up. Figure out what, realistically, can be done about your trial(s) and get busy. If nothing can be done, then realize, as the apostle Paul did, that, "When I am weak, then I am strong."

In regard to physically doing something about a problem, it is important to know that severe (or clinical*) depressions develop physical symptoms that can be treated medically with nonaddicting medi-

---

*A clinical depression is much more severe than a mild "case of the blues." Its symptoms are: decreased sleep, appetite, and energy over an extended period of time.

cation. These depressions intensify the effects of whatever trial we are going through. Of course, spiritual and psychological counseling for such depression is a necessity. Some anxiety disorders also have a treatable physical factor involved. After treatment, there may be a marked decrease in the intensity of whatever trial has triggered the anxiety.

Premenstrual syndrome (PMS) may have a hormonal component that intensifies emotions and makes negative experiences seem much worse. In fact, almost any medical disease will seem to intensify the trials in one's life. With treatment, the intensity of the trials often decreases.

Forgive others and forgive ourselves

In seeing thousands of patients in my psychiatric practice through the years, I have found that a lot of trials are intensified simply by not forgiving others (Eph. 4:31, 32) or one's self (John 1:9; Ps. 103:12–14).

Many times trials are intensified because we are alienated from others who might otherwise be of great help or comfort to us.

I cannot help but wonder if the writer of Hebrews had this in mind when he recorded, "See to it that no one comes short of the grace of God; that no root of bitterness springing up causes trouble, and by it many be defiled" (Heb. 12:15). Indeed, in Ephesians 4:31–32, the apostle Paul recorded the following: "Let all bitterness and wrath and anger and clamor and slander be put away from you, along with all malice. And be kind to one another, tender-hearted, *forgiving each other,* even as God in Christ also has forgiven you" (italics added).

I believe that forgiveness starts with the will. It starts simply by choosing not to hold a grudge. The negative emotions formed from holding a grudge may not change immediately after we choose to forgive. That often takes time and will come later. By choosing to forgive, however, we can avoid depression (anger turned inward). We can ask God to deal with the offending person (Rom. 12:19) and then ask Him to bless that person. Be careful not to tell God how to deal with the other person, however! That's His business.

In psychiatry I have seen two major forces—sociopathy and paranoia—in the refusal to forgive that cause many trials and keep people apart. Sometimes others knowingly treat us wrong (*they* are sociopathic); and sometimes we just think others have treated us wrong (*we* are paranoid). I honestly cannot tell which factor causes the greater amount of trouble.

Therefore, for our own mental health we need to forgive whenever we feel offended, no matter if we think the bad treatment was actual, intentional, nonintentional, or nonexistent except in our own minds. The apostle Paul was preaching good psychological health when he said, "Do not let the sun go down on your anger" (Eph. 4:26b). Paul knew it was important to clear up feelings of anger quickly.

We need to forgive others (Eph. 4:31, 32), and we need to confess our sins to God and to accept His forgiveness. Then we need to forgive ourselves. We must not remain angry with ourselves.

Compare our I.Q. with God's intelligence

I suppose one reason that I have had trouble understanding my trials over the years is simply that I do not have enough intelligence. Oh, sure, I'm smarter than some people. I was smart enough (or at least determined enough) to make it through medical school. But, as much as I hate to admit it, compared to God, my I.Q. (intelligence quotient) is not worth talking about. The Lord declares, "As the heavens are higher than the earth, so are . . . My thoughts [higher than] your thoughts" (Isa. 55:9).

So I can't fully understand God, but I can understand that simple verse found in the Book of Romans, "And we know that God causes all things to work together for good to those who love God, to those who are called according to His purpose" (Rom. 8:28). I know that God is there, that He is in control, and that He somehow will make my trials work for good. It is reassuring to know that God is not picking on me. He is not "out to get me." Rather, He has my best interest at heart. The words He spoke to the children of Israel long ago still are a comfort to God's children today. " 'For I know the plans I have for you,' declares the LORD, 'plans to prosper you and not to harm you, plans to give you hope and a future' " (Jer. 29:11, NIV).

Find our triangle of strength

There is a triangle of strength available only to the children of God. Its three points are Bible knowledge, prayer, and fellow believers. These are emphasized repeatedly throughout Scripture.

1. The Bible gives strength during trials like no other book ever has. It is a book about courageous men and women, danger, success, and victory over trials. Christ said that His words were "spirit" and "life." The apostle John said, "I write to you, young men, because you are strong, and the word of God lives in you" (1 John 2:14b, NIV). Moses described God's Word as our very "life" (Deut. 32:46–47). In Matthew 7:24–25 (NIV), Jesus said: "Therefore everyone who hears these words of mine and puts them into practice is like a wise man who built his house on the rock. The rain came down, the streams rose, and the winds blew and beat against that house; yet it did not fall, because it had its foundation on the rock." In other words, trouble and problems will come, but when we hear and do the Word of God, we will be stable. Truly the Word of God is "quick and powerful" (Heb. 4:12).

2. Prayer helps establish a relationship with God that can withstand any trial. Paul encouraged the Philippians with these words; "Do not be anxious about anything, but in everything, by prayer and petition, with thanksgiving, present your requests to God" (Phil. 4:6, NIV). In Psalm 91:15 God promises: "He will call upon me, and I will answer him." Through prayer God may choose to bless us just as He blessed a rather obscure Old Testament character named Jabez years ago: "Jabez cried out to the God of Israel, 'Oh that you would bless me and enlarge my territory! Let your hand be with me, and keep me from harm so that I will be free from pain.' And God granted his request" (1 Chron. 4:10, NIV).

Truly God wants us to cast all our cares on Him
for He cares for us (1 Peter 5:7). He wants us to know
that He is a stronghold in the "day of trouble" (Nah.
1:7). He wants us to know that nothing is too hard
for Him (Gen. 18:14a). Indeed, we can cry out with
Asaph, "Whom have I in heaven but you? And being
with you, I desire nothing on earth. My flesh and my
heart may fail, but God is the strength of my heart
and my portion forever" (Ps. 73:25, 26, NIV).

3. There is strength in the body of Christ. We do
not have to face trials alone. In 2 Corinthians 1:3, 4
(NIV), the apostle Paul said, "Praise be to the God and
Father of our Lord Jesus Christ, the Father of compassion and the God of all comfort, who comforts us
in all our troubles, so that we can comfort those in
any trouble with the comfort we ourselves have received from God."

In Philippians 2:4 (NIV) he said, "Each of you should
look not only to your own interests, but also to the
interests of others." The wise King Solomon said it
well in Ecclesiastes 4:9–12:

> Two are better than one, because they have a good
> return for their work: If one falls down, his friend
> can help him up. But pity the man who falls and
> has no one to help him up! Also, if two lie down
> together, they will keep warm. But how can one
> keep warm alone? Though one may be overpowered,
> two can defend themselves. A cord of three strands
> is not quickly broken.

I have sometimes found Christians too ashamed to
go to other Christians for help. Remember, all of us

have faults; no one is perfect; no one is without trials. None of us is totally self-sufficient nor does God want us to be. The Bible says that it is better to give than to receive, but *it is not wrong to receive.* If we all refused to receive from others, no one would ever be given an opportunity to give. In fact, allowing others to give to us, *when we have a true need,* is a way of giving to others—giving the opportunity to give.

As the apostle Paul said in Galatians 6, each of us is to carry our own (light or manageable) load or burden (v. 5), but we are also to carry each other's (heavy or overwhelming) burdens (v. 2). When we suffer trials, we may indeed be suffering an overwhelming burden which God wants some friend or neighbor to share. It has been said that a burden shared is only half a burden. How true this is.

Usually we need only to share burdens with a trusted friend but occasionally the nature of the trial is so intense that a professional counselor, a pastor, or Christian psychologist, is needed. This is especially true when any of the following symptoms develop:

sleep disturbance	suicidal feelings
weight disturbance	ongoing headaches
loss of motivation	stomach pain

A Christian professional, one who uses a biblical base to his or her knowledge of human actions and reactions, often can help us alleviate not only the intense feelings resulting from a trial but, from special study and experience, also show us ways to reduce the circumstances of the trial itself.

Take care of our spiritual, physical, and mental concerns

To overcome trials and serve Christ, we must take care of ourselves *spiritually*. "Rid yourselves of all malice and all deceit, hypocrisy, envy, and slander of every kind. Like newborn babies, crave pure spiritual milk, so that by it you may grow up in your salvation. . . . Abstain from sinful desires, which war against your soul. Live such good lives among the pagans that . . . they may see your good deeds and glorify God on the day he visits us" (1 Peter 2:1–2, 12, NIV).

To overcome trials and serve Christ, we must also, as much as possible, take care of ourselves *physically*. We may have all the desire in the world to serve Him, but if we have no energy, as a result of poor physical care, we will be unable to reach the potential He intended for us.

To overcome trials and serve Christ, we must also take care of ourselves *mentally or psychologically*. Our mental diet is extremely important. Be careful of what you allow into your mind, particularly the media's constant debasing perversion of humanity. We were created in God's image to glorify Him. Therefore we need to concentrate on positive ways of thinking and looking at life, avoiding approval or even passive commitment to material that causes us to value ourselves and humanity as less than what we were intended to be.

For years researchers wondered why people got high when they took drugs. In order for drugs to work, there had to be receptors in the brain to which they could attach. These receptors were probably meant for another purpose and in recent years this purpose has been discovered. It is possible for the body to produce its own "uppers," called endorphins, which attach themselves to these receptors and produce a natural feeling of well-being. These endorphins are produced when we think positive, happy thoughts. Therefore it is possible, when we focus our minds on the positive things of Christ and the Christian life, to actually become "high on Christ."

Our brain is an enormously complex computer that records most of what we see and hear, although not all images are recorded to the same degree of intensity. Our brain plays back its "computer tapes" constantly, telling us, often subconsciously, how to react and respond to various situations. If we have had bad "programming," it is harder for us to respond and react positively. The less reprogramming we have to do of these bad tapes, the better.

The Book of 1 Peter was written to Christians who because of persecution had fled to Asia Minor. They were still suffering as exiles because they lived in a pagan and unfamiliar world which also persecuted them. Peter tells those Christians how to react to suffering. Again and again he admonishes them to overcome their suffering by preparing "your minds for action; be self-controlled . . . be clear minded and self-controlled so that you can pray. . . . Be self-controlled and alert. Your enemy the devil prowls around like a roaring lion looking for someone to devour. Resist him, standing firm in the faith" (1 Peter 1:13; 4:7; 5:8, 9, NIV).

Most Christians never accomplish what God intended for them because they neglect one of these three areas: the physical, the spiritual, or the mental/psychological. In both 1 Peter 5 and Ephesians 6, we are shown that we have an enemy, Satan, who is out to get us. He is devious and will so cleverly seduce us that we won't even realize our ability to glorify God has been diminished. No matter how and why our trials began, we will not be able to overcome their circumstances and/or their resulting feelings if we don't keep a healthy body, a healthy spirit, and a healthy mind.

Realize God's presence with us

We are never alone. God has said: "I will never leave thee, nor forsake thee" (Heb. 13:5, KJV). What a comfort to know that we never have to face any trial alone. Our friend, our Savior, our Lord, is always there.

I can still see in my mind's eye the expression of comfort on my friends' faces as they sang the following old hymns in the little country church I attended as a youth.

The Lily of the Valley

I've found a friend in Jesus, He's everything to me,
He's the fairest of ten thousand to my soul!
The "Lily of the Valley," in Him alone I see

All I need to cleanse and make me fully whole:
In sorrow He's my comfort, in trouble He's my stay:
He tells me every care on Him to roll;
He's the "Lily of the Valley," the Bright and Morning
　Star;
He's the fairest of ten thousand to *my* soul!

　　　　　　　　　　　　　　　　　C.W. Fry

Never Alone

When in affliction's valley,
I'm treading the road of care,
My Saviour helps me to carry
My cross when heavy to bear,
My feet entangled with briars,
Ready to cast me down;
My Saviour whispered His promise,
Never to leave me alone.

God is there with "chariots of fire."

There is a very interesting and intriguing story told in 2 Kings 6:15–17. The godly prophet Elisha and his young disciple found themselves facing a seemingly insurmountable trial.

When the servant of the man of God got up and went out early the next morning, an army with horses and chariots had surrounded the city. "Oh, my lord, what shall we do?" the servant asked. "Don't be afraid," the prophet answered. "Those who are with us are more than those who are with them." And Elisha prayed, "O LORD, open his eyes so he may see." Then the LORD opened the servant's eyes, and he looked and saw the hills full of horses and chariots of fire all around Elisha.

Obviously we do not have chariots of fire around us to protect us constantly, but we do have the strength of God. We are His; He is our father. He loves us with an incomprehensible love. Indeed, He is always there in every trial and tribulation. We may often be unaware of the unseen protection which surrounds us. Nevertheless, it *is* there!

10

Reasons for Trials

Although our response to suffering is much more important than knowing the reason or reasons for it, the Bible does give a number of reasons for suffering, one or more of which may apply to a particular trial we are facing. If we cannot easily and certainly determine which reason applies to a specific situation, however, it is best just to wait for God to reveal this, if and when He chooses to do so.

From my psychiatric observations, it seems that we bring many troubles on ourselves but fail to realize it (of course, God is in control and allows us to suffer the fruits of our own actions).

The following list enumerates the reasons for suffering given in the Bible that I have found and memorized over the years. You may find others.

1. To produce character and hope

Therefore, since we have been justified through faith . . . we rejoice in the hope of the glory of God. Not only so, but we also rejoice in our sufferings, because we know that suffering produces perseverance; perseverance, character; and character, hope. And hope does not disappoint us, because God has poured out his love into our hearts by the Holy Spirit, whom he has given us.

Romans 5:1–5, NIV

2. *To produce endurance and completeness*

Consider it pure joy, my brothers, whenever you face trials of many kinds, because you know that the testing of your faith develops perseverance. Perseverance must finish its work so that you may be mature and complete, not lacking anything.

James 1:2–4, NIV

3. *To show the power of Christ*

Three times I pleaded with the Lord to take it away from me. But he said to me, "My grace is sufficient for you, for my power is made perfect in weakness." Therefore I will boast all the more gladly about my weaknesses, so that Christ's power may rest on me. That is why, for Christ's sake, I delight in weaknesses, in insults, in hardships, in persecutions, in difficulties. For when I am weak, then I am strong.

2 Corinthians 12:8–10, NIV

4. *To show the glory of God*

As he went along, he saw a man blind from birth. His disciples asked him, "Rabbi, who sinned, this man or his parents, that he was born blind?"

"Neither this man nor his parents sinned," said Jesus, "but this happened so that the work of God might be displayed in his life."

John 9:1–3, NIV

5. *To show what faith can do*

A woman was there who had been subject to bleeding for twelve years. She had suffered a great deal under the care of many doctors and had spent all she had, yet instead of getting better she grew worse. When she heard about Jesus, she came up behind him in the crowd and touched his cloak, because she thought, "If I just touch his clothes, I will be healed." Immediately her bleeding stopped and she felt in her body that she was freed from her suffering.

At once Jesus realized that power had gone out from him. He turned around in the crowd and asked, "Who touched my clothes?"

"You see the people crowding against you," his disciples answered, "and yet you can ask, 'Who touched me?' "

But Jesus kept looking around to see who had done it. Then the woman, knowing what had happened to her, came and fell at his feet and, trembling with fear, told him the whole truth. He said to her, "Daughter, your faith has healed you. Go in peace and be freed from your suffering."

Mark 5:25–34, NIV

6. *To learn to depend on God*

We do not want you to be uninformed, brothers, about the hardships we suffered in the province of Asia. We were under great pressure, far beyond our ability to endure, so that we despaired even of life. . . . But this happened that we might not rely on ourselves but on God.

2 Corinthians 1:8, 9, NIV

7. *To be able to comfort others in their trials*

Praise be to the God and Father of our Lord Jesus Christ, the Father of compassion and the God of all comfort, who comforts us in all our troubles, so that we can comfort those in any trouble with the comfort we ourselves have received from God.

2 Corinthians 1:3, 4, NIV

8. *To show the "proof" of faith*

Praise be to the God and Father of our Lord Jesus Christ! In his great mercy he has given us new birth into a living hope through the resurrection of Jesus Christ from the dead, and into an inheritance that can never perish, spoil or fade—kept in heaven for you, who through faith are shielded by God's power until the coming of the salvation that is ready to be revealed in the last time. In this you greatly rejoice, though now for a little while you may have had to suffer grief in all kinds of trials. These have come so that your faith—of greater worth than gold, which perishes even though refined by fire—may be proved genuine and may result in praise, glory and honor when Jesus Christ is revealed. Though you have not seen him, you love him; and even though you do not see him now, you believe in him and are filled with an inexpressible and glorious joy, for you are receiving the goal of your faith, the salvation of your souls.

1 Peter 1:3–9, NIV

9. *Because of a ministry for Christ*

Are they Hebrews? So am I. Are they Israelites? So am I. Are they Abraham's descendants? So am

I. Are they servants of Christ? (I am out of my mind to talk like this.) I am more. I have worked much harder, been in prison more frequently, been flogged more severely, and been exposed to death again and again. Five times I received from the Jews the forty lashes minus one. Three times I was beaten with rods, once I was stoned, three times I was ship-wrecked, I spent a night and a day in the open sea, I have been constantly on the move. I have been in danger from rivers, in danger from bandits, in danger from my own countrymen, in danger from Gentiles; in danger in the city, in danger in the country, in danger at sea; and in danger from false brothers. I have labored and toiled and have often gone without sleep; I have known hunger and thirst and have often gone without food; I have been cold and naked. Besides everything else, I face daily the pressure of my concern for all the churches.

2 Corinthians 11:22–28

10. To keep down pride

I must go on boasting. Although there is nothing to be gained, I will go on to visions and revelations from the Lord. I know a man in Christ who fourteen years ago was caught up to the third heaven. Whether it was in the body or out of the body I do not know—God knows. And I know that this man—whether in the body or apart from the body I do not know, but God knows—was caught up to Paradise. He heard inexpressible things, things that man is not permitted to tell. I will boast about a man like that, but I will not boast about myself, except about my weaknesses. Even if I should choose to boast, I would not be a fool, because I would be speaking the truth. But

I refrain, so no one will think more of me than is
warranted by what I do or say.

To keep me from becoming conceited because of
these surprisingly great revelations, there was given
me a thorn in my flesh, a messenger of Satan, to
torment me.

2 Corinthians 12:1–7, NIV

As in the case of Job, Satan desired to attack Paul's
body, to keep him from praising God for all the wonderful things that had been revealed to him. However, what Satan meant for evil, God meant for good
and used it to remind Paul that he was not super-
human and more special than others. He could not
expect to be "the Teacher's pet," protected from all
suffering.

11. Because of irresponsible behavior by others

The Book of Hosea tells us, in summary, that Hosea's wife was a prostitute. She caused him much
grief. He remained a godly man who suffered many
trials because of another's sin and irresponsible
behavior.

12. Because we are part of a fallen race and world

Many trials that we suffer are just part of being
human, a descendant of Adam's sinful race, and have
little to do with specific sins, punishments, or pur-
poses for our individual lives.

He [the Lord God] said, . . .
Have you eaten from the tree that I commanded you
not to eat from?"

The man said, "The woman you put here with me—she gave some fruit from the tree, and I ate it."

Then the LORD God said to the woman, "What is this you have done?"

The woman said, "The serpent deceived me, and I ate."

. . . To the woman he [the Lord] said,

"I will greatly increase your pains in childbearing;
    with pain you will give birth to children.
Your desire will be for your husband,
    and he will rule over you."

To Adam he said, "Because you listened to your wife and ate from the tree about which I commanded you, 'You must not eat from it,'

    "Cursed is the ground because of you;
        through painful toil you will eat of it
        all the days of your life.
    It will produce thorns and thistles for you,
        and you will eat the plants of the field.
    By the sweat of your brow
        you will eat your food
    until you return to the ground,
        since from it you were taken;
    for dust you are
        and to dust you will return."

Genesis 3:11–13, 16–19, NIV

13. Because we reap what we sow

Do not be deceived: God cannot be mocked. A man reaps what he sows. The one who sows to please his sinful nature, from that nature will reap destruction; the one who sows to please the Spirit, from the Spirit will reap eternal life.

Galatians 6:7, 8, NIV

Reaping is the natural result of sowing the seed which produces that particular crop. If we sow bad seed the bad crop or trials are a natural result of those sinful actions, something we should have realized would naturally result.

14. For discipline

"My son, do not make light of the Lord's discipline,
and do not lose heart when he rebukes you,
because the Lord disciplines those he loves,
and he punishes everyone he accepts as a son."

Endure hardship as discipline; God is treating you as sons. For what son is not disciplined by his father? If you are not disciplined (and everyone undergoes discipline), then you are illegitimate children and not true sons. Moreover, we have all had human fathers who disciplined us and we respected them for it. How much more should we submit to the Father of our spirits and live! Our fathers disciplined us for a little while as they thought best; but God disciplines us for our good, that we may share in his holiness. No discipline seems pleasant at the time, but painful. Later on, however, it produces a harvest of righteousness and peace for those who have been trained by it.

Hebrews 12:5–11, NIV

15. Because of the sovereignty of God

God is in control of this earth and universe. No one else can decide who should or should not suffer or when the trials should come. God can choose to give trials or victories to whom he wills.

All the peoples of the earth are regarded as nothing.
He does as he pleases with the powers of heaven and
the peoples of the earth.
No one can hold back his hand or say to him: "What
have you done?"

Daniel 4:35, NIV

No one from the east or the west or from the desert
can exalt a man.
But it is God who judges:
He brings one down, he exalts another.

Psalm 75:6, 7, NIV

16. Our enemy, Satan, seeks to destroy us

Our struggle is not against flesh and blood, but
against the rulers, against the authorities, against
the powers of this dark world and against the spiritual forces of evil in the heavenly realms.

Ephesians 6:12, NIV

Your enemy the devil prowls around like a roaring
lion looking for someone to devour.

1 Peter 5:8, NIV

One of those persons Satan wished "to devour"
was Simon Peter. Christ told Peter this before it happened. "Simon, Simon, Satan has asked to sift you
as wheat" (Luke 22:31, NIV). Note that Satan did not
have the power to attack Peter without asking God's
permission first. God was still in control.

When Peter voiced his allegiance to Jesus, He told
him that "before the rooster crows today, you will
deny three times that you know me" (Luke 22:34,
NIV).

Satan wished to destroy Simon Peter's faith, because it was being used to greatly magnify God and could be used to magnify Him more in the future.

When we are having an effective ministry for the Lord or we are on the verge of magnifying Him in some special way, we should not consider it unusual to run into obstacles, particularly if those obstacles would cause us to believe that God couldn't use us.

Sometimes our heavy problems may come not because we have done something wrong (as a discipline from God), but because we have done something right. And because of our potential to magnify God, Satan wants to destroy us.

What should we do when Satan seeks to destroy us?

Take Paul's advice to:

Put on the whole armor of God so that you can take your stand against the devil's schemes.

Put on . . .
the belt of truth . . .
the breastplate of righteousness . . .
your feet fitted with the readiness that comes from
  the gospel of peace. . . .
the shield of faith . . .
the helmet of salvation, and
the sword of the Spirit, which is the word of God.

And pray in the Spirit on all occasions.

Ephesians 6:11, 14–18, NIV

Be self-controlled and alert. . . . Resist [the devil], standing firm in the faith.

1 Peter 5:8, 9, NIV

What can we expect when we resist the devil?

Resist the devil, and he will flee from you. Come near to God and he will come near to you.

James 4:7, 8, NIV

What can we expect if we do not resist the devil?

Even though we started out right, we may succumb to the temptations of Satan. If we do, we can know two things:

1. Jesus, the mediator between God and man, prays for us, as he did for Simon, "But I have prayed for you, Simon, that your faith may not fail" (Luke 22:33a, NIV).

2. Jesus expects us to turn again to Him and to go on to magnify Him even more, "And when you have turned back, strengthen your brothers" (Luke 22:33b, NIV).

Having denied his Lord three times out of fear and confusion, Peter went on to become the great apostle of Christianity. From Jesus' words to Peter in Luke 22:33, we know that He understands our weaknesses and that, when we fail Him, we can still turn again to Him and have our lives magnify Him perhaps even more than they did before.

Jesus considered it best to tell Peter of his coming temptation from Satan. In Job's case God did not tell him either before or after his sufferings why they came. This leads us to our final consideration regarding our sufferings.

17. *Reason known to God but not given to man*

One day the angels came to present themselves before the LORD, and Satan also came with them. The LORD said to Satan, "Where have you come from?"

Satan answered the LORD, "From roaming through the earth and going back and forth in it."

Then the LORD said to Satan, "Have you considered my servant Job? There is no one on earth like him; he is blameless and upright, a man who fears God and shuns evil."

"Does Job fear God for nothing?" Satan replied. "Have you not put a hedge around him and his household and everything he has? You have blessed the work of his hands, so that his flocks and herds are spread throughout the land. But stretch out your hand and strike everything he has, and he will surely curse you to your face."

The LORD said to Satan, "Very well, then, everything he has is in your hands, but on the man himself do not lay a finger."

Then Satan went out from the presence of the LORD.

One day when Job's sons and daughters were feasting and drinking wine at the oldest brother's house, a messenger came to Job and said, "The oxen were plowing and the donkeys were grazing nearby, and the Sabeans attacked and carried them off. They put the servants to the sword, and I am the only one who has escaped to tell you!"

While he was still speaking, another messenger came and said, "The fire of God fell from the sky and burned up the sheep and the servants, and I am the only one who has escaped to tell you!"

While he was still speaking, another messenger came and said, "The Chaldeans formed three raiding parties and swept down on your camels and carried them off. They put the servants to the sword, and I am the only one who has escaped to tell you!"

While he was still speaking, yet another messenger came and said, "Your sons and daughters were feasting and drinking wine at the oldest brother's house, when suddenly a mighty wind swept in from the desert and struck the four corners of the house. It collapsed on them and they are dead, and I am the only one who has escaped to tell you!" At this, Job got up and tore his robe and shaved his head. Then he fell to the ground in worship and said:

"Naked I came from my mother's womb,
    and naked I will depart.
The LORD gave and the LORD has taken away;
    may the name of the LORD be praised."
In all this, Job did not sin by charging God with
    wrongdoing.

Job 1:6–22, NIV

Some trials we can avoid; others we cannot. For those trials we can't avoid, God's grace will be sufficient. Even when trials are our fault, because of His gracious kindness, His grace will still be sufficient. We only have to ask Him to be with us and to carry us through.

11

Comfort from an Old Hymn Book

I have an old hymn book, so worn over the years that the paper is fragile and the covers are held together by a thread. This old hymnal is filled with songs that give help and comfort in times of trials. I have tried to analyze these songs to determine why they are so helpful. I believe it is because they:

1. contain biblical messages, and God always honors that.
2. utilize repetition. The brain mainly records what it hears repeated over and over.
3. give a simple but profound message. Again, the brain more easily records simple but profound messages in its biochemical memory bank.
4. are personal. The brain records personal fears, anxieties, and trials; but it also records stories of faith, love, and hope in these trials. Such is the message of these songs. I have picked out a few that have given help to me.

Face to Face

Carrie E. Breck

Face to face with Christ my Savior,
Face to face—what will it be?
When with rapture I behold Him,
Jesus Christ who died for me?
Only faintly now I see Him,
With the darkened veil between,
But a blessed day is coming,
When His glory shall be seen.

What rejoicing in His presence,
When are banished grief and pain;
When the crooked ways are straightened,
And the dark things shall be plain.

Face to face! O blissful moment!
Face to face—to see and know;
Face to face with my Redeemer,
Jesus Christ who loves me so.
Chorus:
Face to face I shall behold Him,
Far beyond the starry sky;
Face to face in all His glory,
I shall see Him by and by!

For now we see through a glass, darkly; but then
face to face.

1 Corinthians 13:12, KJV

A Reflection

A few years ago I began to see Christ more and
more as my best friend. Just the thought of someday
seeing Him face to face decreases the intensity of my
trials.

Tell It to Jesus

Jeremiah E. Rankin

Are you weary, are you heavy-hearted?
Tell it to Jesus, tell it to Jesus;
Are you grieving over joys departed?
Tell it to Jesus alone.
Tell it to Jesus, tell it to Jesus,
He is a friend that's well known;
You've no other, such a friend or brother,
Tell it to Jesus alone.

Do the tears flow down your cheeks unbidden?
Tell it to Jesus, tell it to Jesus;
Have you sins that to men's eyes are hidden?
Tell it to Jesus alone.
Tell it to Jesus, tell it to Jesus,
He is a friend that's well known;
You've no other such a friend or brother,
Tell it to Jesus alone.

Do you fear the gathering clouds of sorrow?
Tell it to Jesus, tell it to Jesus;
Are you anxious what shall be tomorrow?
Tell it to Jesus alone.
Tell it to Jesus, tell it to Jesus,
He is a friend that's well known;
You've no other such a friend or brother,
Tell it to Jesus alone.

Are you troubled at the thought of dying?
Tell it to Jesus, tell it to Jesus;
For Christ's coming kingdom are you sighing?
Tell it to Jesus alone.
Tell it to Jesus, tell it to Jesus,
He is a friend that's well known;
You've no other such a friend or brother,
Tell it to Jesus alone.

And the apostles gathered themselves together unto
Jesus, and told him all things, both what they had
done, and what they had taught. And he said unto
them, Come ye yourselves apart into a desert place,
and rest a while.

                                        Mark 6:30, 31, KJV

A Reflection

I disagree with sharing trials *only* with Jesus. He
wants us to also share with other Christians. But
what powerful words, otherwise! Perhaps only those
who have been through heavy trials can feel the
emotion of this song.

The Rock That Is Higher Than I

E. Johnson

O sometimes the shadows are deep,
And rough seems the path to the goal,
And sorrows, sometimes how they sweep
Like tempests down over the soul!

O sometimes how long seems the day,
And sometimes how weary my feet;
But toiling in life's dusty way,
The Rock's blessed shadow, how sweet!

O near to the Rock let me keep,
If blessings or sorrows prevail;
Or climbing the mountain way steep,
Or walking the shadowy vale.

Chorus:
O then to the Rock let me fly,
To the Rock that is higher than I;
O then to the Rock let me fly,
To the Rock that is higher than I!

When my heart is overwhelmed: lead me to the rock
that is higher than I.

Psalm 61:2, KJV

A Reflection

Many troubled souls have found great comfort in
picturing Christ as a Rock, a fortress on a high, rocky
cliff or hill, to which they can escape and rest from
the stress of life's tribulations.

What a Friend

Joseph M. Scriven

What a Friend we have in Jesus,
All our sins and griefs to bear!
What a privilege to carry
Everything to God in prayer!
O what peace we often forfeit,
O what needless pain we bear,
All because we do not carry
Everything to God in prayer!

Have we trials and temptations?
Is there trouble anywhere?
We should never be discouraged,
Take it to the Lord in prayer.
Can we find a friend so faithful
Who will all our sorrows share?
Jesus knows our every weakness,
Take it to the Lord in prayer.

Are we weak and heavy-laden,
Cumbered with a load of care?
Precious Savior, still our refuge,
Take it to the Lord in prayer.
Do thy friends despise, forsake thee?
Take it to the Lord in prayer;
In His arms He'll take and shield thee,
Thou wilt find a solace there.

Be careful for nothing; but in every thing by prayer and supplication with thanksgiving let your requests be made known unto God. And the peace of God, which passeth all understanding, shall keep your hearts and minds through Christ Jesus.

Philippians 4:6, 7 KJV

A Reflection

All too often we bear needless emotional pain because we fail to recognize that we have a friend, Jesus Christ, who wants to talk, not only to us but also with us. He is truly interested in us and in our trials.

Amazing Grace

John Newton

Amazing grace! How sweet the sound
That saved a wretch like me!
I once was lost, but now am found,
Was blind, but now I see.

'Twas grace that taught my heart to fear,
And grace my fears relieved;
How precious did that grace appear
The hour I first believed!

**Through many dangers, toils, and snares,
I have already come;
'Tis grace hath brought me safe thus far,
And grace will lead me home.**

When we've been there ten thousand years,
Bright shining as the sun,
We've no less days to sing God's praise
Than when we'd first begun.

I commend you to God, and to the word of his grace,
which is able to build you up, and to give you an
inheritance among all them which are sanctified.

Acts 20:32, KJV

A Reflection

I find it hard to add thoughts to this old favorite.
I was a sinner by birth and by choice (a "wretch")
but I was also of tremendous worth to God—enough
so that He sent His Son to die for me. That's *amazing
grace*! He also stands by me in my trials. That, too,
is amazing grace.

Just as I Am

Charlotte Elliott

Just as I am, without one plea,
But that Thy blood was shed for me
And that Thou bidd'st me come to Thee,
O Lamb of God, I come, I come.

Just as I am, and waiting not
To rid my soul of one dark blot,
To Thee whose blood can cleanse each spot,
O Lamb of God, I come, I come.

Just as I am, though tossed about
With many a conflict, many a doubt,
Fightings and fears within, without,
O Lamb of God, I come, I come.

Just as I am, poor, wretched, blind;
Sight, riches, healing of the mind.
Yea, all I need in Thee to find,
O Lamb of God, I come, I come.

Just as I am! Thou wilt receive,
Wilt welcome, pardon, cleanse, relieve,
Because Thy promise I believe,
O Lamb of God, I come, I come.

But God commendeth his love toward us, in that, *while we were yet sinners*, Christ died for us (italics added).

Romans 5:8, KJV

A Reflection

The greatest trial in life actually is not poor circumstances but not knowing Christ. I am glad He accepted me just as "I am" so that He could "rid my soul of one dark blot."

Rock of Ages

Augustus M. Toplady

Rock of Ages! cleft for me,
Let me hide myself in Thee;
Let the water and the blood
From Thy wounded side which flowed.
Be of sin the double cure,
Save from wrath, and make me pure.

Could my tears forever flow,
Could my zeal no languor know,
These for sin could not atone.
Thou must save, and Thou alone;
In my hand no price I bring,
Simply to Thy cross I cling.

While I draw this fleeting breath,
When my eyes shall close in death,
When I rise to worlds unknown,
And behold Thee on Thy throne,
Rock of Ages! cleft for me!
Let me hide myself in Thee.

Lead me to the rock that is higher than I.

Psalm 61:2, KJV

A Reflection

Many a dear saint through the years has found
comfort in trials from a sense of hiding in the cleft
of the Rock.

I Need Thee Every Hour

Annie S. Hawks
Robert Lowry, Chorus

I need Thee every hour, most gracious Lord;
No tender voice like Thine can peace afford.

I need Thee every hour, stay Thou near by;
Temptations lose their power when Thou art nigh.

I need Thee every hour in joy or pain;
Come quickly and abide or life is vain.

I need Thee every hour, Most Holy One;
O make me Thine indeed, Thou blessed Son!

Chorus:
I need Thee, O I need Thee;
Every hour I need Thee;
O bless me now, my Savior,
I come to Thee!

> . . . your Father knoweth what things ye have need
> of, before ye ask.
>
> Matthew 6:8, KJV

> . . . my God shall supply all your need according to
> his riches by Christ Jesus.
>
> Philippians 4:19, KJV

A Reflection

Indeed, I need Christ every hour, in joy or pain.
The immediacy of the song makes it strong.

Sweet Hour of Prayer

William W. Walford

Sweet hour of prayer! sweet hour of prayer!
That calls me from a world of care,
And bids me at my Father's throne
Make all my wants and wishes known;
In seasons of distress and grief,
My soul has often found relief,
And oft escaped the tempter's snare,
By thy return, sweet hour of prayer!

Sweet hour of prayer! sweet hour of prayer!
Thy wings shall my petition bear
To Him whose truth and faithfulness
Engage the waiting soul to bless;
And since He bids me seek His face,
Believe His Word and trust His grace,
I'll cast on Him my every care,
And wait for thee, sweet hour of prayer!

Sweet hour of prayer! sweet hour of prayer!
May I thy consolation share,
Till, from Mount Pisgah's lofty height,
I view my home, and take my flight:
This robe of flesh I'll drop and rise
To seize the everlasting prize;
And shout, while passing through the air,
Farewell, farewell, sweet hour of prayer.

Now Peter and John went up together ... at the hour of prayer.

Acts 3:1, KJV

A Reflection

Let's face it. I live in a world of care. This hymn implies a regular time of prayer, a time when one is lifted above earthly trials and cares.

I personally feel very fortunate in that although I have had "cares," I also have been blessed. However, many persons cannot say that. For them the "seasons of distress" are overwhelming. Prayer offers a solitude, a getting-away-from-it-all, a sense of relief, a hope that things will change, an avenue of guidance, and sometimes even a sense of what to do and what to expect to see that change come about.

Higher Ground

Johnson Oatman, Jr.

I'm pressing on the upward way,
New heights I'm gaining every day;
Still praying as I onward bound,
"Lord, plant my feet on higher ground."

My heart has no desire to stay
Where doubts arise and fears dismay;
Though some may dwell where these abound,
My prayer, my aim, is higher ground.

I want to live above the world,
Though Satan's darts at me are hurled;
For faith has caught the joyful sound,
The song of saints on higher ground.

I want to scale the utmost height,
And catch a gleam of glory bright;
But still I'll pray till heaven I've found,
"Lord, lead me on to higher ground."

Chorus:
Lord, lift me up and let me stand,
By faith, on heaven's tableland,
A higher plane than I have found;
Lord, plant my feet on higher ground.

Set your affection on things above, not on things on
the earth.

Colossians 3:2, KJV

A Reflection

Many Christians over the centuries who were facing "doubts, fears, Satan's darts," and trials have suc-
ceeded by keeping their eyes on "higher ground."

Leaning on the Everlasting Arms

Elisha A. Hoffman

What a fellowship, what a joy divine,
Leaning on the everlasting arms;
What a blessedness, what a peace is mine,
Leaning on the everlasting arms.

Oh, how sweet to walk in this pilgrim way,
Leaning on the everlasting arms;
Oh, how bright the path grows from day to day,
Leaning on the everlasting arms.

What have I to dread, what have I to fear,
Leaning on the everlasting arms?
I have blessed peace with my Lord so near,
Leaning on the everlasting arms.

Chorus:
Leaning, leaning,
Safe and secure from all alarms;
Leaning, leaning,
Leaning on the everlasting arms.

The eternal God is thy refuge and underneath are
the everlasting arms.

Deuteronomy 33:27, KJV

A Reflection

Is all this possible?

> what a fellowship
> how sweet to walk
> what a joy
> how bright the path
> safe and secure from all alarms

No doubt the godly man who wrote this had known his share of trials. Yes, all this is possible in Christ.

'Tis so Sweet to Trust In Jesus

Louisa M. R. Stead

'Tis so sweet to trust in Jesus,
Just to take Him at His word;
Just to rest upon His promise,
Just to know, "Thus saith the Lord."

O how sweet to trust in Jesus,
Just to trust His cleansing blood;
Just in simple faith to plunge me
'Neath the healing, cleansing flood!

**Yes, 'tis sweet to trust in Jesus,
Just from sin and self to cease;
Just from Jesus simply taking
Life and rest, and joy and peace.**

I'm so glad I learned to trust Thee,
Precious Jesus, Savior, Friend;
And I know that Thou art with me,
Wilt be with me to the end.

Chorus:
Jesus, Jesus, how I trust Him!
How I've proved Him o'er and o'er!
Jesus, Jesus, precious Jesus!
O for grace to trust Him more!

. . . because we trust in the living God, who is the
Saviour of all men.

1 Timothy 4:10, KJV

A Reflection

Somehow, in wrestling with trials, it is easy to lose
the rest, and joy, and peace. I need to be reminded
to trust in Jesus.

O, How I Love Jesus

Frederick Whitfield

There is a name I love to hear,
I love to sing its worth;
It sounds like music in my ear,
The sweetest name on earth.

It tells me of a Savior's love,
Who died to set me free;
It tells me of His precious blood—
The sinner's perfect plea.

It tells me what my Father hath
In store for every day,
And though I tread a darksome path,
Yields sunshine all the way.

It tells of One whose loving heart
Can feel my deepest woe,
Who in each sorrow bears a part,
That none can bear below.

Chorus:
O, how I love Jesus,
O, how I love Jesus,
O, how I love Jesus,
Because He first loved me!

We love him, because he first loved us.

1 John 4:19, KJV

A Reflection

There is something about the name of Jesus that causes a deep calm within my heart.

Ready

Charlie D. Tillman

Ready to suffer grief or pain,
Ready to stand the test;
Ready to stay at home and send
Others, if He sees best.

Ready to go, ready to stay,
Ready to watch and pray;
Ready to stand aside and give,
Till He shall clear the way.

Ready to speak, ready to think,
Ready with heart and brain;
Ready to stand where He sees fit,
Ready to stand the strain.

Ready to speak, ready to warn,
Ready o'er souls to yearn;
Ready in life, ready in death,
Ready for His return.

Chorus:
Ready to go, ready to stay,
Ready my place to fill;
Ready for service, lowly or great,
Ready to do His will.

... be ready always to give an answer to every man that asketh you a reason of the hope that is in you with meekness and fear.

1 Peter 3:15, KJV

A Reflection

It must have taken a brave person to pen this song—one who was even ready for trials, if that was in God's plan!

Hallelujah Square

I saw a blind man, tapping along,
Losing his way as he passed thru the throng;
Tears filled my eyes,
I said, "Friend, you can't see,"
With a smile on his face, he replied to me.

I'll see all my friends in Hallelujah Square,
What a wonderful time we'll all have up there;
We'll sing and praise Jesus,
His glory to share,
And you'll not see one blind man in Hallelujah
  Square.

Now I saw a cripple, dragging his feet,
He couldn't walk like we do down the street;
I said, "My friend, I feel sorry for you,"
But he said, "Up in heaven
I'm gonna walk just like you."

I'll see all my friends in Hallelujah Square,
What a wonderful time we'll all have up there;
We'll sing and praise Jesus,
His glory to share,
And you'll not see one cripple in Hallelujah Square.

Now I saw an old man, gasping for breath,
Soon he'd be gone as his eyes closed in death;
He looked at me, said,
"Boy, don't look so blue,
I'm going up to heaven, how about you?"

I'll see all my friends in Hallelujah Square,
What a wonderful time we'll all have up there;
We'll sing and praise Jesus,
His glory to share,
And we'll all live forever in Hallelujah Square.

> For our conversation [citizenship] is in heaven; from
> whence also we look for the Saviour, the Lord Jesus
> Christ: Who shall change our vile body, that it may
> be fashioned like unto his glorious body, according
> to the working whereby he is able even to subdue
> all things unto himself.
>
> Philippians 3:20, 21

A Reflection

Many Christians have physical trials from which
they have little hope of recovery. However, someday
those trials will disappear: the blind will see; the
lame will walk; and the deaf will hear.